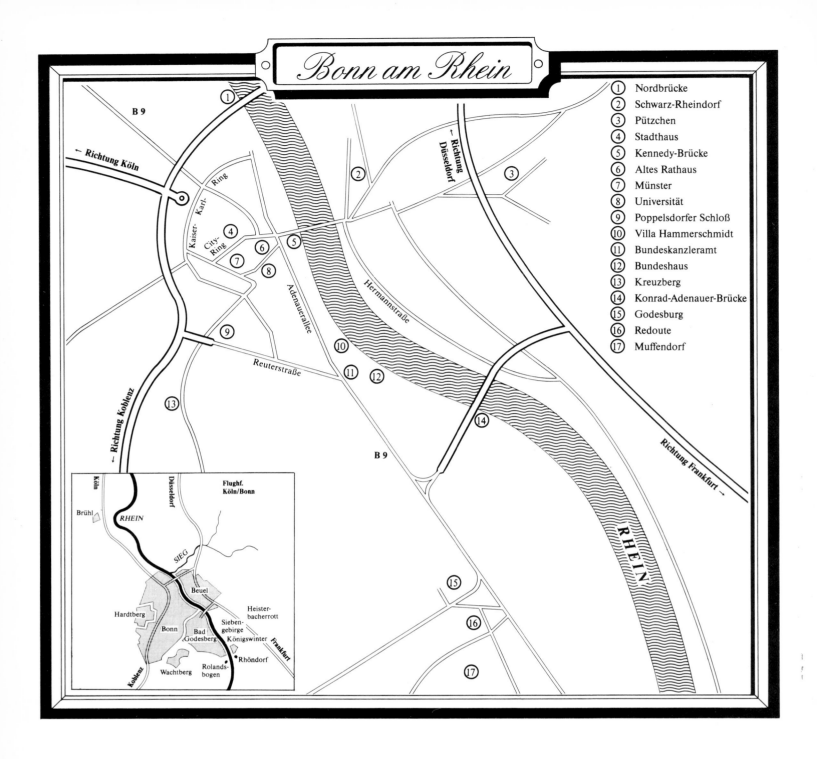

Bonn am Rhein

1. Nordbrücke
2. Schwarz-Rheindorf
3. Pützchen
4. Stadthaus
5. Kennedy-Brücke
6. Altes Rathaus
7. Münster
8. Universität
9. Poppelsdorfer Schloß
10. Villa Hammerschmidt
11. Bundeskanzleramt
12. Bundeshaus
13. Kreuzberg
14. Konrad-Adenauer-Brücke
15. Godesburg
16. Redoute
17. Muffendorf

Fotografie: Bernd Siering, Thomas Thelen · Text: Erhard Schoppert

© 1988 **Parkland Verlag, Stuttgart**

Cover lay-out: Klaus Pachnicke
Type-setting: Siering KG, Bonn
Translation: Una Tomašević

ISBN 3-88059-339-6

BONN

Bonn
The four city-districts

People used to laugh and joke about it, call the 'little town in Germany', 'deader than a Chicago cemetery', and claim that it was the only capital with no night-life worth mentioning. Eventually, they learned to value and love the provisional capital, the city which in forty years has won itself an unmistakeable capital-city image and its place in the world.

Naturally, the 2000-year-old Bonn, which came into the spotlight of world history only in 1948 with the founding of the Federal Republic of Germany, cannot be measured against cities such as Cologne or Düsseldorf, Frankfurt or Berlin. From the point of view of size and history, this tranquil town on the Rhine is not to be compared with Rome, Paris or London. The boldest statisticians cannot push the number of inhabitants up to 300,000 even when they include all the diplomats. The city fathers themselves have seized on other attributes in order to compete in the international stakes. Among those who are interested only in superlatives, Bonn has finally found its place as the greenest European capital — not in the political sense, but because of its many parks and meadows, its woods and farmland.

Of the 141 square kilometres which make up the Bonn district, almost half is green. Some 25 square kilometres, mostly on the right bank of the Rhine, are used for agriculture, and over 40 are forest. Looking down over the city from the surrounding heights, such as the Godesberg, or from the Town Hall, one is struck by the number of tree-lined avenues, thanks to which much of the 15 square kilometres of streets lie under a shadowy green vault.

The present city of Bonn was formed in 1969 by the inclusion of Beuel, Bad Godesberg and parts of the Duisdorf district in the metropolitan area. It thus now consists of four city districts: Bonn with 64.2 square kilometres, Bad Godesberg with 32, Beuel with 33.1 and Hardtberg with 11.9. However, these formerly independent towns did not join Bonn quite freely and willingly. The garden, spa and diplomatic city of Bad Godesberg, in particular, put up a bitter resistance and only gave in when the Superior Administrative Court of Münster confirmed the decision. Since then the Bonn lion has also flown on the Godesburg keep. The lion as the emblem of the city was taken from a Roman statue of a lion slaying a boar. Popularly called the 'stone wolf', in the Middle Ages it stood in the Münsterplatz as a symbol of justice. Today it can be seen in the entrance hall of the old Town Hall in the Marktplatz. Although in the 19th century it used to be a red lion on a blue background, following the municipal reorganization, in 1971 the city colours became red-gold-red — a kind of concession to the inhabitants of Bad Godesberg, whose colours were red and gold. The black cross on a silver ground was already a common feature of the emblems of the two towns, as it was the coat-of-arms of the electors of Cologne.

Despite all attempts at unification, the visitor will soon realise that this commune consists of no fewer than 40 villages joined together. Each has preserved its own centre, celebrates its own feasts and leads a separate life despite the district administration and

City Council. When a Dottendorfer hops on a tram for a 20-minute ride to the inner city, he has not only 'travelled to the city', but also passed through the village of Kessenich and Poppelsdorf. A Lannesdorfer usually means the Godesberg Theaterplatz when he says he is 'going into town'. If he travels by train or car in the direction of the Münsterplatz or the Marktplatz, he still calls this a 'trip to Bonn'.

It is no wonder, then, that the 70-metre-high glass Town Hall is among the least-loved buildings in Bonn — and not only because of its exterior. Controversial from the very beginning, and considered by many to be an eye-sore, it is now admitted to be an architectural *faux pas* of the late Seventies and is grumblingly endured. Since then the 'monstrosity on the Rhine' has even acquired a positive aspect: the beautifully restored 19th-century façades around it are reflected in its windows. However, the burgers rarely need to enter this thousand-windowed den of the lion, since offices for day-to-day business have been opened in the former town halls of almost all the suburbs.

The old Town Hall, which closes off the eastern side of the triangular Marktplatz, is today the setting for many official receptions. Particularly eye-catching are the double flights of steps of the building designed by Michael Leveilly on the site of the former mediaeval building. It was from here, in the revolutionary year of 1848, that Gottfried Kinkel and Karl Schurz spoke to the crowd, the black-red-gold banner in their hands; here, in 1949, Theodor Heuss adressed the people as the first Federal President, and Charles de Gaulle, John F. Kennedy and Queen Elizabeth II appeared after signing the Golden Book of the city in the Gobelin hall. Each year the carnival prince receives the ovations of his subjects on this spot.

Above left, the old Town Hall with the coat-of-arms on the mansard roof and below it the clock held by satyrs; below left, the old city emblem from the time before Bad Godesberg, Beuel and Duisdorf were joined to Bonn; above right, the unloved new Town Hall with the glass façade; below, the 'stone wolf', a Roman statue which served as model for the Bonn lion.

Bad Godesberg

When, after the choice of Bonn as provisional capital, its international recognition slowly followed, Bad Godesberg, which had largely been spared wartime destruction, started attracting the diplomats streaming to the Rhine. Thus the garden, spa and congress city also became a diplomatic city. Of the 113 embassies at present in Bonn, 81 have their official premises in what is now the city district of Bad Godesberg. To these are added four more missions of countries with which the Federal Republic of Germany has a 'special relationship', such as the German Democratic Republic. About 3,600

of the total 7,150 diplomats accredited to Bonn live around the Godesburg.

Not surprisingly, then, the market in this quarter is a very lively, colourful place, with Chinese and Africans side by side buying fruit and vegetables, and the Eifel dialect mingling with American English. Gone are the days when the locals stopped to stare at an Indian woman in a sari, and Africans and Arabs in their traditional robes. The shops in the area long ago began catering for the diplomats' special requirements. Even the gastronomy is international.

Many of the old villas of the former 'Pensionopolis', where retired people of means settled at the turn of the century because of the mild climate, today serve as embassy buildings or ambassadorial residences. The existing buildings, however, could not meet all the requirements, and in the Fifties whole embassy complexes sprang up. The build-

ings of the US embassy stand on stilts for protection against high water in the Mehlem 'Deichmanns Aue'. At Plittersdorf, the US colony has its own shopping centre, cinema, swimming-pool and school as well as the Stimpson memorial chapel with its slim white spire, built in 1953 in the New-England style.

The People's Republic of China took over the ruined Rigal'sche palace in the Kurfürstenallee and rebuilt it as its embassy, cleverly combining Rhineland brick and oriental pagoda roofs. Even the two stone lions at the impressive main gate fit into the setting.

In the Kurpark (spa park), among beautiful trees, stands the Stadthalle. Constructed in 1955 and enlarged several times, it has an international reputation as a congress centre. The gatherings held here include meetings of the NATO countries' foreign ministers, the

Central Committee of German Catholics, and the Christian and Free Democrats. This hall also witnessed the framing of the famous Godesberg SPD programme, long before the Greens celebrated their entry into the Bundestag in the same building.

La Redoute, only a stone's throw away, provides a splendid setting for state receptions. Between 1790 and 1792 it was built for the holding of balls given by the electoral princes. Today hardly an official visit passes without a reception in its stately rooms.

Above left, the Bad Godesberg Redoute, the diplomatic 'stamping ground' of the federal capital; below, the embassy of the People's Republic of China in the former Rigal'sche palace; above right, Godesburg keep with the state flag and coat-of-arms of Greater Bonn, formed in 1969 out of four municipalities.

Hardtberg and Beuel

The western city district of Hardtberg was formed in 1969 by a communal reorganisation. The best-known establishment here is certainly Hardthöhe, the seat of the Ministry of Defence. Hardtberg underwent rapid development in the 70's and 80's. On the Brüser Berg hill, also called the 'Bonn balcony', some 10,000 new flats were constructed in the largest residential project undertaken by the state of North Rhine-Westphalia. The rural idyll of half-timbered houses mingles here with modern buildings in a variety of forms and materials. A large sculpture by the Haus Rücker Co. art group, with its airy construction, standing in the Borsigallee in the centre of this housing development, was intended to define the essence of architecture. The Bonn inhabit-

ants found their own definition for another housing estate: because of its box-like appearance from a distance, they named the Medinghoven development 'Legoland'. Medinghoven takes its name from a neo-Gothic castle.

The inhabitants of Hardtberg are envied for their infrastructure and good facilities: among other things, they have open-air and indoor swimming pools with a fine view of the Cologne bay. The Kottenforst close by also improves the quality of life.

The western parts of Bonn have an additional attraction because of their altitude. While the Bonn climate is often sticky and muggy because of the city's low-lying position, humidity, and certain urban building errors which have obstructed the free flow of air currents, the climate is much pleasanter at an altitude. This fact induces ever more Bonn inhabitants to turn their backs on the valley and move to higher suburbs, and even nearby villages.

One undesirable consequence of this is traf-

fic congestion, which has led to Hardtberg being intersected by two broad arteries: the 565 motorway running westward to the Voreifel and the Konrad-Adenauer avenue, a very heavily laden north-south stretch through the city.

From the early Middle Ages to the early 20th century, wine was produced in Duisdorf and Lengsdorf. The Phylloxera epidemic which decimated vines throughout the north Rhineland's vine-growing regions, put an end to vineyards here. An old wine press on the square before the parish church of St Peter in Chains at Lengsdorf is a reminder of those times, as are the annual wine festivals. The wide distribution of federal ministries and agencies is also evident in Duisdorf. Large areas are occupied by the Ministries of Food, Agriculture and Forestry, Labour and Social Security, and Economic Affairs. A shopping precinct and pedestrian zone have been created in Rochusstrasse. The cemetery in the Bahnhofstrasse has a memorial to 102 Soviet soldiers who died in the

Duisdorf prisoner-of-war camp during World War II.

Beuel lies on the right bank of the Rhine, on the 10-kilometre stretch between the mouth of the Sieg in the north and the Siebengebirge in the south, and extends seven kilometres eastwards. The eastern bank of the Rhine was settled by the Romans, probably in order to safeguard the river crossing for Bonn. In 1809 Napoleon made a market town out of 13 adjoining villages which had a considerable amount of manufacturing, but Beuel did not gain a charter until 1952. The town's coat of arms, commemorating those times, depicts a ferry and 13 stars. Beuel is considered the cradle of the Rhineland's traditional carnival day on which women assume control, a tradition inaugurated by the washerwomen of Beuel 150 years ago. On the Thursday before the actual carnival weekend, Beuel becomes the headquarters of the colourfully costumed women. In many places laundry is hung up on flag-staffs as a sign that on this day

housewives give up their work and join in the merriment. The Beuel women chose their joke ruler, the washerwoman-princess, who reigns until Ash Wednesday, moving from festive hall to festive hall and accepting the homage of the people. The three villages of Limperich, Kündinghoven and Ramersdorf crown their own carnival royalty, the 'LIKURA' princess. Tie-wearers should avoid encountering any 'Wiewer', as they are called in the Rhineland, as many among them are armed with scissors and collect ties as trophies. Anyone who tries to defend himself at the sight of a pair of scissors becomes extremely unpopular.

No less colourful are the festivities in late summer at the 'Pützchens Markt', the most important market-fair of the Rhineland. Together with the Munich Oktoberfest, the Hamburg Dom and the Canstatt Wasen, it counts among the greatest festivals in Germany.

The alternative cultural scene of the capital has found a 'home' in a former bread factory

in Beuel. All contemporary trends in the visual and performing arts are represented here, and it is now not only the 'scene' which gathers here and moves, after the show, to the nearby inn for discussions. The theatre has also established workshops in a disused jute mill, and has a rehearsal stage which can also be used for performances. The Youth Theatre likewise has its premises in Beuel. In the Catholic parish church of St Joseph, regular organ recitals are held. The tower of this neo-Gothic brick building houses a carillon of 62 bells.

Left the unnamed statue in the Brüger Berg housing estate which defines the essence of architecture; **Above** "Pützchens Markt", the largest fair in the Rhineland, every year attracts hundreds of thousands of people to right-bank Bonn.

7

Around Bonn

Hardly any town in Germany can compete with Bonn in the beauty of its location: sky-piercing mountains, ancient fortified towns and monasteries, forests, undulating hills, cornfields, orchards and vineyards; on top of this, the most beautiful University buildings that any such institution can show.' With these words of praise the poet Ernst Moritz Arndt enthused about his chosen home town in 1830. Whoever has the good fortune to view the valley of the Rhine from one of the tall buildings in the government quarter will still be able to relate to this panagyric. At the juncture of the Lower and Central Rhine, Bonn offers, to the south, the incomparable panorama of the Siebengebirge ('seven hills'). This northwestern end of the Westerwald has over 30 peaks in all, though it is the seven that stand out on the northern side that gave the chain of hills its name. These are Drachenfels, Wolkenburg, Lohrberg, Grosser Ölberg, Nonnenstromberg, Petersberg and Löwenburg. The most famous are the Drachenfels, often jokingly called the highest hill in the Netherlands, and Petersberg, whose hotel is well-known as the government guesthouse. The Queen of England stayed here, as well as the Soviet Party leader Leonid Brezhnev, who during his official visit gave the security forces a headache by trying out his new German limousine on the steep, winding approach to the hotel at an earlier hour than planned.
Opposite the Siebengebirge lie the foothills of the Eifel with the Rodderberg and Rolandsbogen. Within the city area of Bad

Godesberg are the basalt peak and keep of Godesburg, the northernmost bastion of the Rhineland hill-top castles. Behind it stretches the green rolling countryside of the Drachenfels Ländchen. Tucked away in this mostly agricultural area there are many romantic moated castles. Visible from afar is the radio telescope with a parabolic mirror of the Research Association for Applied Natural Sciences, which is used for satelite observation. The well-known Adendorf potteries were established in the 17th century, when potters moved here from the Westerwald.

To the north, the Rhine valley opens out into the Cologne bay. A sweeping view extends across the Sieg flats, before which stands the Michaelsberg in Siegburg with a Benedictine abbey of the same name.

In the west, beyond the Venusberg, Voreifel and Ville, stretch the Vorgebirge, on whose slopes the ancient Romans built their villas. The Vorgebirge is considered to be the market garden of the capital.

Some 22 kilometeres northwest of Bonn lies the town of Brühl with the Augustusburg palace, today often used by the federal government as a splendid setting for state banquets.

Above, the stunning panorama of the Siebengebirge; below left, a rural scene in the Bonn area. On the right-hand page, the interior of Brühl palace; below, the moated Gudenau castle by Wachtberg-Villip.

Romans, the French and the Prussians
The History of Bonn

It is often said that wherever one may dig, an ancient Roman will spring out of the earth. It is, indeed, true that, wherever an excavator is being used, scholars keep a sharp eye on it. Frequently the work must be stopped in mid-course to leave the area to the archaeologists of the Rheinisches Landesmuseum (Rhine Regional Museum). They are still uncovering evidence of the country's history, always connected with changes of power, wars and destruction. The Romans, the Franks and the Wittelsbachs came, the French and the Prussians had their say, the Americans and the British moved in, and finally also the federal authorities. They all left their mark which is impressed, more or less distinctly, on the city of today.

Precisely when the Romans built the first fort in the area, probably taking the name of the place from the Celts, is not known. The true age of the town is still a matter of argument among historians. The Roman legionaries' camp *Castra Bonnensia* to the north of the present city was first mentioned by Tacitus in AD 69. It was destroyed during the Batavi uprising and eventually replaced by stone fortifications. The northern gate of the Roman camp is today marked by a cast of the legionary Claudius's gravestone.

For about 400 years the Romans camped here, leaving abundant stone testimony of their presence before they were eventually driven out by the Franks. The latter, together with the population which remained behind, inhabited the *Bonnburg* and built the first church, Dietkirchen. The remains of this edifice, discovered only in the 1970s, are now part of a little 'archaeological park' located in the middle of the Römerkastell housing estate.

Before the arrival of the Franks, Cassius and Florentius, two members of the Theban Legion who became Christians, are supposed to have died a martyr's death here for refusing to accord the emperor divine honours and to take part in the persecution of Christians. Cassius and Florentius are still the city's patrons. As early as AD 300, a *cella memoria* was raised on the presumed site of their graves and in around 400 a little church, which is supposed to have been founded by St. Helena. Today, this spot, around which the present city centre arose at the turn of the millennium, is marked by the massive Münster (cathedral). Archaeological excavations in the Münster in 1930 indicated that this was a Roman temple district, which shows how many stone monuments were left by the Romans. The cult of the Auphanian matrons, female deities, was particularly popular in Bonn.

Near the Münster the St. Cassiusstift abbey was raised, with the *villa Basilica* settlement, and next to it a trading quarter, named *vicus Bonnensis,* developed on the area of the present-day Marktplatz.

Roman and Frankish relics: above left, gravestone of the legionary Claudius; below, stone relief of the Frankish church at the Römerkastell; right, the *Matronensteine* (figures of female deities) found during excavations in the Münster.

MATRONIS
AVFANIABVS
QVETTIVS · SEVERVS
QVA

In the early Middle Ages Bonn, together with Lotharingia, became a part of the German Empire (925). In this period the Emperors Otto II and Henry II briefly honoured the city with their presence. The entry of Bonn into the Empire was arranged in 921 by Kings Henry I and Charles the Simple on a ship named 'Lotharingia', which lay at anchor in Bonn. The *villa Basilica* was turned, towards the end of the 10th and beginning of the 11th centuries, into a *Stiftsburg* (episcopal town). The St. Cassiusstift flourished around the middle of the 12th century under the provost Gerhard von Are and large parts of the Münster and the monastery buildings were raised.

The Sterntor gate is a relic of the building activities of the 13th century, and originally stood at the end of the Sternstrasse. In 1898 it was moved to the Bottlerplatz square and built onto the Halbrundturm tower of the former city walls.

Bonn was first burnt down in 1198, during the campaign of King Philip of Swabia against Otto the Guelph and Archbishop Adolf of Cologne. It went up in flames again in 1239, during the struggle of the Archbishops of Cologne and the Dukes of Brabant for supremacy in the region between the Rhine and the Maas, to which also the cor-

Above left, the copy of the Gothic Hochkreuz, next to it the Alte Zoll, part of the former city walls. Right, the pillory at the Münster; On the right-hand page above, the attack led by the mercanary leader Martin Schenk von Nideggen in 1587; below, the Sterntor gate.

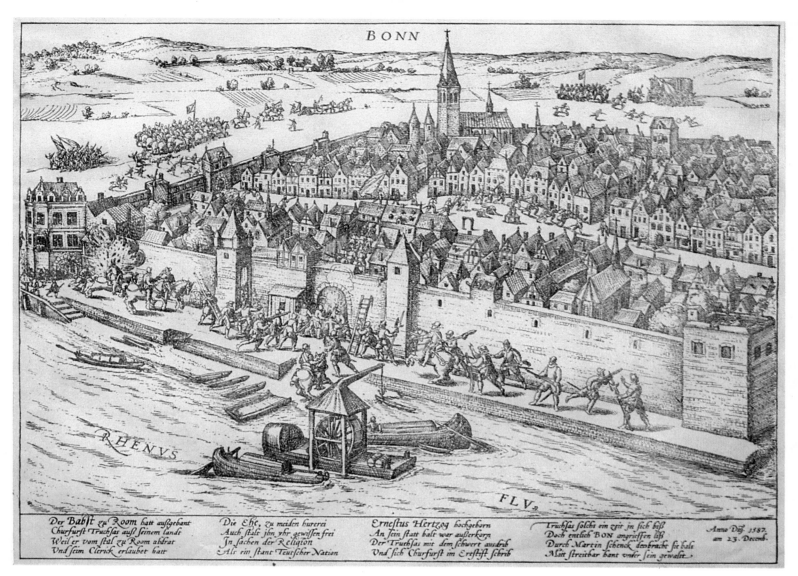

BONN

RHENVS

FLV.

Der Babst zu Room hatt ausgebant | Die Ehe, zu meiden hurerei | Ernestus Hertzog hochgeborn | Truchsas solchs ein zeit in sich liß | Anno Dñi 1587.
Churfurst Truchsas auß seinem landt | Auch stalt ihn yhr gewissen frei | An sein statt bald war außerkorn | Doch entlich BON angriessen liß | am 23. Decemb.
Weil er vom stal zu Room abtrat | In sachen der Religion | Der Truchsas mit dem schwert außtrib | Durch Martin schenck deobrachte sie bald
Vnd sein Clerick erlaubet hatt | Als ein stant Teutscher Nation | Vnd sich Churfurst im Erestift schrib | Mit streitbar hant vnder sein gewalt

The construction of the Poppelsdorf palace was begun in 1715, according to the plans of the Parisian architect de Cotte and the Bonn construction engineer Hauberath, by the Elector Joseph Clement on the site of a mediaeval moated castle. It was completed between 1730 and 1753 under the Elector Clement Augustus.

onation city of Aachen belonged. Konrad von Hochstaden (1236—61) finally ordered walls to be built around the city and gave the inhabitants rights and freedom. The electoral princes of Cologne, not very popular with the inhabitants of their city, started more frequently to reside in Bonn.

At this time the Münsterplatz was called the 'Grosser Hof' and also served as the lawcourt. Today the old pillory stands on the spot where the law-court was built onto the Münster: evil-doers were clamped by neckirons to the shaft of the Roman pillar and given over to public abuse. The trachyte ball

on the top of the pillar of shame symbolises the world and the sovereignty of the judges. The 11-metre tall Gothic stone cross on the old Römerstrasse (Roman road) between Bonn and Godesberg also dates from the Middle Ages; many legends are connected with this striking landmark. In 1981, the original was moved to the Landesmuseum because of the effects of air pollution and the vibrations from the nearby motorway. A copy of the Hochkreuz was raised not far from its original location.

The impact of Martin Luther's new teachings was also felt in the Rhineland. In 1542 the archbishop-elector of Cologne, Hermann von Wied, tried to introduce Protestantism in the region with the help of the Strasbourg reformer Martin Bucer, but was deposed. Later Archbishop Gebhard Truchsess von Waldburg, wishing to marry, adopted the new faith, this resulting in his replacement as archbishop by Ernest of Bavaria and the

'Cologne War', in which Ernest's troops occupied and plundered Bonn in 1583. The Godesberg palace, built in 1210, was destroyed during the war.

Electoral Prince Ferdinand carried out the Counter-Reformation, founded numerous monasteries and finally moved his court completely to Bonn. His successors fortified the city, a remnant of which is the Alter Zoll on the Rhine. After three sieges and destruction by Brandenburg troops in 1689, in 1715 the fortifications were razed to the ground at the instigation of the Netherlands. This was fortunate for posterity, for it permitted Elector Joseph Clement to build palaces in Bonn and Poppelsdorf and so lay the foundations in Bonn of the Baroque style which is still prominent in the town centre. His successor, Clement Augustus, completed the princely residence. The magnificence of this court brought prosperity to the citizens and an upsurge of artistic and cultural activities. Much

of the electoral palace was destroyed by a fire in 1777.

In 1794 the last electoral prince to reside in Bonn, Max Francis, a son of Empress Maria Theresa, raised the academy founded in 1777 by his predecessor to the level of a university. Two years later he had to flee from the advancing French revolutionary troops. Bonn was annexed to France as part of the Rhine-Mosel Department between 1798 and 1814, during which period the university was suppressed.

In 1815 the Prussians entered the town and turned Bonn into a garrison city. After a fierce conflict with Cologne, the Friedrich-Wilhelms-Universität was founded in 1818. After World War I the city experienced first British, then French occupation, which lasted until 1926. The Pedagogical Academy was founded in the same year. Several bombing raids during World War II caused extensive destruction, among other things al-most completely razing the mediaeval city centre.

A new chapter began in 1948, after the military governors of the three western zones permitted the prime ministers of the states in these zones to form a constituent assembly. This assembly, the Parliamentary Council, met in Bonn in order to work out a constitution for the newly-formed state. The president was Konrad Adenauer, who later became the first Chancellor of the Federal Republic of Germany. The fact that he had his own house in nearby Rhöndorf, at the foot of the Drachenfels, influenced the decision to make Bonn the temporary seat of the federal government. On November 3, 1949, the newly-elected Bundestag (lower house of the West German Parliament) decided that Bonn should become the 'provisional' capital of the country. Frankfurt had also been an option at the time.

Bonn was thus confronted by quite new tasks and needs which completely changed the face of the city. Accommodation for ministries and organisations, the mass media and embassies had to be built, and the city spread way beyond its former boundaries. New motorways and transport facilities had to be provided and whole areas, even in neighbouring towns, were cleared to obtain the necessary space. In 1969 an urban planning law was passed which also covered the towns of Bad Godesberg and Beuel, as well as parts of the region of Duisdorf and the Siegkreis. A year later, the Federal Republic of Germany, North Rhine-Westphalia and the city of Bonn came to a financial agreement about the planned building of Bonn as the capital, thereby ending the temporary political arrangement.

The Power on the Rhine
Politics in Bonn

Nowhere else do the old, tranquil little town of the 19th century and the capital of a modern industrial state come closer together than in the government quarter of Bonn. The epochs intermingle and — as is only natural — often conflict. The Alexander Koenig Zoological Museum became famous after World War II as the site of the opening session of the Parliamentary Council, which was held in its central hall, among numerous stuffed beasts, on September 1, 1948. The giraffe, towering above all, was a silent witness of the proceedings and the formation of a new Germany, as not enough cloth was found to cover its long neck.

Diagonally opposite, on the Rhine side of the Adenauerallee lie the Villa Hammerschmidt — the seat of the Federal President, the Palais Schaumburg, and the modern Federal Chancellery. Until 1979 the Palais Schaumburg, situated in a large park, served as the Chancellery. Today it is the guesthouse of the Federal Presidents and Chancellors. The multi-winged building was constructed between 1858 and 1860 by a prosperous citizen named Loeschigk. In 1891 it became the property of Prince Adolf of Schaumburg-Lippe and his wife, Princess Victoria of Prussia, a sister of William II. In 1949 the bulding became the Federal Chancellery, having passed ten years earlier into the ownership of the state. A carefully conceived annex dates from Chancellor Adenauer's time.

The functional new office of the Chancellor was built a little further south, at a cost of over 100 million marks, between 1974 and 1976. Here, over 400 employees in 240 rooms carry out the orders of the Chancellor, who sets the guidelines of the country's policies. The Chancellor's wing is set slightly apart and connected to the main building by a two-storey bridge. The forecourt is dominated by a monumental sculpture by the British artist Henry Moore, entitled 'Two Large Forms'. It was placed there in 1979, and two years later bought at the request of Helmut Schmidt, then the Federal Chancellor.

Below, right, the central hall of the Alexander Koenig Museum; above the Federal Chancellery with the Henry Moore statue; bottom, the Chancellery and the Federal Press and Information Office — a bird's-eye view. Following pages: the guest house of the Federal Presidents and Chancellors, the Palais Schaumburg.

The Villa Hammerschmidt, often called the 'White House on the Rhine', was built between 1863 and 1865, and reconstructed in 1878 by Leopold Koenig, the father of zoologist Alexander Koenig, who also had the ten-acre park laid out. The Federal Republic of Germany acquired the estate from the heirs of the distinguished businessman Rudolf Hammerschmidt, and turned it into the office of the Federal President, whose standard, a black eagle on a gold background with a red border, is always raised when the President is in residence.

While the Chancellor and his officials obtained a purpose-built domicile some years ago, the legislature was obliged to move from one provisional home to another. A temporary plenary hall was arranged in an old waterworks near the Bundeshaus (Federal Parliament Building). The new plenary hall should offer the representatives more comfort.

The assembly hall of the former Pedagogical Academy had already been used by the Parliamentary Council before the Bundesrat (upper house of the West German Parliament) held its meetings there. The building was constructed from 1930 to 1933 in the clear-cut forms of Bauhaus architecture, a style that was officially frowned upon at the time of the building's completion. Even before Bonn became the capital, the Academy began to be reconstructed as a parliament building. The plenary hall overlooking the Rhine was larger than the former Reichstag, and offered space for at least 518 members. The seats were arranged in a semi-circle, with the members of the presidium sitting in the front, under the Federal Eagle and behind the speakers's desk; to their left are the members of the Federal Government, to their right the members of the Bundesrat. Some 350 seats were planned for guests, diplomats and journalists.

A vast number of reporters have set up camp around the Bundeshaus. All larger foreign agencies have their own offices, the larger newspapers their own correspondents who question the politicians at federal press conferences. The Government's Federal Press and Information Office is responsible for the flow of information both into and out of the Bundeshaus.

The Federal Press Office, with over 700 employees and a huge technical apparatus is responsible for the flow of information in and out of the building. Foreign news is received here in over 20 languages, more than 70 television and radio programmes are constantly monitored, and some 30 news agencies send information to the Press Office. To this are added German and foreign magazines and newspapers, which are all analysed here. From all this are compiled the eight-page briefing given to the Chancellor every day, several hundred pages of commentary, and information files for various ministries and some 50 other recipients in the government domain which are all supplied with information by the Press Office.

On the left-hand page, banners in front of the office of the Federal Chancellor; above, the red carpet before the new Federal Chancellery; below, a motorcycle escort; left, guard of honour formed of the Federal Border Guards.

Foreign missions obtain important information from this centre via a television, radio and teleprinter network. Data on over 35,000 important living and historic personalities are stored in the archives.

In addition, the Federal Press Office is also the 'largest travel agency' in the capital. By this is meant the Visitors' Service, which annually looks after 70,000 visitors. Each member of the Bundestag can invite up to 100 inhabitants from his constituency on two annual information trips. To this are added groups which visit the city as guests of the federal government. For the hotel and restaurant business they constitute a major factor, as every fifth hotel in Bonn is provided with guests by the Federal Press Office. This amounts to some 150,000 overnight stays and 200,000 meals per annum in the 100 hotels and restaurants on the list of the Visitors' Service. This brings in some 17 million marks a year.

Very close to the Bundeshaus is the 112-metre-tall 'Lange Eugen' building which houses the offices of the members of the Bundestag, their assistants and employees. The 30-storey building was named after the former Bundestag President Eugen Gerstenmeier, who initiated the construction of the building.

For the inhabitants of Bonn, flags and bunting have long become a common sight, whether they are pennants on government or diplomatic vehicles, or street decorations during official state visits. During the World Economic Summit meeting, the old plenary hall of the Bundeshaus, which served as the venue, was decorated with the banners of all the nations taking part. Flags are also flown on embassies and other diplomatic buildings, while colourful coats-of-arms allow the initiated to recognise what mission they be-

Above, the front of the Villa Hammerschmidt; below, the front garden; on the right-hand page the Blue Gobelin Hall in the seat of the Federal President.

long to at first sight. Others, however, will
have to take a closer look.

During the early years of the Federal Republic, guests of state used to arrive by train. Today, the Cologne-Bonn airport provides the
fastest connection, especially as the administrative district is linked to it by a direct motorway. Naturally, on such official occasions
the red carpet is also rolled out, and signing
the Golden Book of the city of Bonn is almost always in the programme. Meeting the
crowds, a 'ceremony' in which many state
guests used to readily participate, has for
security reasons become a rare occasion.
Not surprisingly, alongside all this, another
manifestation of democracy is also present:
demonstrations. The inhabitants of Bonn
sometimes grumble at having to pay the
price for gloating over Frankfurt in 1949.

On the limits of the city district of Bad Godesberg a new Post Office Ministry building
has been raised, together with modern accommodation for the Federal Ministries of
Justice, Education and Science, and Research and Technology. Sheep can still be
seen grazing on as yet unused, although already planned, areas of the Federal district.
With the so-called 'Bonn-Vertrag' (Bonn
agreement) between the city, the Federal
Republic of Germany and the state of North
Rhine-Westphalia, the provisional political
status came to an end. However, the provi-

**Above, the former Plenary Hall of the Bundestag;
right, the provisional hall in the former waterworks
building; far right, a demonstration, with the
'Lange Eugen' building in the background.**

24

sional accommodation situation, with the dispersal of the administration over more than 70 different buildings, will last until the completion of the planned construction of the city according to the agreement. In this context, communications networks are just as important as ministry buildings. Gigantic projects, such as the building of city-rail and car tunnels under Bad Godesberg's inner city will turn Bonn into a building site past the year 2,000. Apart from the government buildings, a history museum and the Bundeskunsthalle (Federal Arts Hall) are planned, aimed at making the former provincial town an international art metropolis.

As a result of these measures, numerous diplomatic missions are also developing their activities and building residences, consular and embassy buildings. Similar to the

25

US colony in Plittersdorf, on the heights above Bad Godesberg the Soviets have created their own little town with a shopping centre, cinema and swimming-pool.
Unfortunately, because of the increasing threat of terrorism and the ever-tighter security, the view of many architecturally interesting buildings is now blocked by walls or thick hedges which conceal the barbed wire surrounding the buildings. Many diplomatic premises can now be entered only after rigorous checks.

Many official banquets and receptions are held in Bonn and its surroundings. On the left-hand page, above, a New Year reception given by the Federal President in the Beethoven Hall of the Bad Godesberg Redoute; below, the Baroque staircase of Brühl palace, designed by Balthasar Neumann. On the right-hand page, above, Queen Elizabeth II's walkabout in the Marktplatz; below, Arab diplomats in traditional robes in front of La Redoute; left, the former Hotel Petersberg, due to be reconstructed as a government guest-house. Small illustration, above, the colourful coat-of-arms of a diplomatic mission.

On the following two pages, a bird's eye view of the inner city of Bonn; right, the Münster and square; left, the Marktplatz and Town Hall; above, the University and lawns.

The University

The University, grown to over 30.000 students, has permeated the whole city with its institutes, student accommodation and pubs. The electoral palace has remained the focal point of the Alma Mater. The central part of the building has a square tower at each corner, and includes sections of the former palace, destroyed in 1689. At the end of the 17th and the beginning of the 18th centuries, Electoral Prince Joseph Clement raised the present building, designed by the Munich architect Zuccalli. The central courtyard reveals the Italian inspiration. Between the towers on the northern side is the main entrance, facing the city centre.

Political unrest forced the prince into exile in Paris. On his return, he enlarged the palace from 1715 to 1723. The southern wing was aligned with the Clemensruh pleasure palace in Poppelsdorf, built in 1715. There was formerly a French-style garden on the site of the present University lawns, surrounded by trees.

The palace gardens today serve not only as a lawn for students to relax on, but as the setting for large demonstrations, watched over,

so to speak, by the Regina Pacis statue, placed above the southern gate of the University. This gilded lead figure survived both the great palace fire in 1777 and the bombing in 1944. Today it is the emblem of the University.

When the palace fire broke out on January 15, 1777, it was so bitterly cold in Bonn that there was no water to extinguish it, and the blaze raged for three days. The citizens felt malicious glee at the fact that the Electoral Prince Maximilian Frederick, a notorious miser, managed to escape in nothing but his shirt.

The east wing of the palace was rebuilt after the fire in a simpler style, without the mansard roof, while the west wing was not reconstructed until the 1920s, only to burn again, together with the whole building, in 1944. The next rebuilding took place in the 1960s. Also worth seeing is the palace chapel, built after the first fire in Louis XVI style. At the behest of Frederick William IV, from 1817 it served the Evangelical community. Today it is the place of worship of Evangelical students, and because of its fine acoustics is often used for concerts and functions.

The Gallery building, raised between 1751 and 1755 by Clement Augustus, stretches to the very banks of the Rhine and closes off the old town to the south like a large yellow

wedge. The third floor houses the collection of the Ethnology Institute, with exhibits from all over the world. The clean lines of the Gallery wing are broken by the structure of the Michaelstor gate, which originally served as an archive and meeting place for the Order of St. Michael. The figure of the Archangel which today adorns the Michaelstor is a copy of an older gilded lead statue. This Baroque gate, like the palace wing, was built by the city architect M. Leveilly with the cooperation of Fr. Cuvilies. The city side is ornamented with bas-reliefs, while the façade towards the palace gardens has Ionic and Doric columns. The coat-of-arms, cartouches, statues and lantern tower on the roof make the Michaelstor a striking city gate, through which passes the busy Adenauerallee, leading to theatres, the Beethovenhalle and Kennedy bridge.

Knowledge and amusement are not mutually exclusive, although research, study and

Above, the long Gallery wing of the University with the Michaelstor; next to it, the Michaelstor with a copy of a 1730 statue; right, the central part of the former electoral palace, today the main University building, flanked by massive towers.

classes take up most of the professors' and
students' time. On one occasion, the Bonn
students made a relief representing a 'Roman Bacchanalia' and presented it as a ge-
nuine archaeological find. This practical
joke was soon found out, and today the relief is built into a wall on the bank of the
Rhine near the Beethovenhalle.

At the Max Planck Institute for Radio-as-
tronomy things are more serious. For the
purpose of 'eavesdropping' on distant stars,
an enormous radio-telescope has been raised
near Effelsberg. The more down-to-earth Zo-
ology and Mineralogy Institutes share the
Poppelsdorf palace. The Mineral-Petrology
Museum, arranged in 1818 when the University was established, is well worth a visit.
The palace was destroyed during the war
and rebuilt in a simpler style, combining the
circle and the square: the square building
with corner pavilions encloses a circular ar-
caded courtyard. By the construction of an
additional storey on the north wing, some of
the roof structure, on whose design Balthasar Neumann worked, was lost.

**Above, the inner courtyard of the Poppelsdorf pa-
lace; on the right the radio-telescope of the Max
Planck Institute in Effelsberg; far right, 'Roman
Bacchanalia', a student joke.**

CASTRIS PER ALEMANNOS CAPTIS VLVLANDVM
EST ROMANIS CVM LVPIS VEL POTIVS VVLPIBVS

Behind the Poppelsdorf palace, which is surrounded by a moat, are the Botanical Gardens of the University, with hothouses for tropical plants, which in 1819 replaced the old palace gardens.

West of the Poppelsdorf palace begins the Nussallee, which was originally planned to exted as far as Brühl, but was never completed. Numerous natural science institutes are grouped here, among others the Agricultural Faculty, founded in 1845 as a college, and the Chemistry Institute. At the time it was built, in 1864 to 1867, the latter was considered the largest and most modern institute building in the world. In front of the building stands a statue, raised in 1903, of the founder of organic chemistry, August Kekulé, who lived and worked in Bonn from 1865 to 1896. The structure of benzine is his most famous discovery. A representation of the benzine ring adorns the parapet of the statue by Hans Everding, while the sphynxes on the sides represent eternity. The statue was paid for by donations from the chemical industry and admirers of the scientist, Emperor William II among them.

The former Soenneken office materials and stationary factory, now restored, houses further institutes. The founder, Friedrich Soenneken of Remscheid, invented and developed not only rounded cursive lettering and round-tipped pens, but also articles still in use, such as letter files, punches and turnover calendars.

To the south of the palace gardens are the Akademische Kunstmuseum, the University Library and the Juridikum (Law School). The library was raised between 1958 and 1960 on the site of the demolished building of the 'Lese' society, which played an important role in the cultural life of the city. Behind the two-storey administration wing, the building stretches towards the Rhine with only one storey. The reading rooms are in a one-storey wing built around a central hall. In front of the University stands a sculpture by Hans Arp ('Wolkenschale'), made of Ticino marble and weighing three tons. Near the Library are the Beethoven-Gymnasium and the St. Cyprianskirche, the episcopal church of the Old Catholics. Its tower spans the pavement.

On the opposite side of the street is the captivating façade of the Juridikum. The wall-decorations of enamel by the Hungarian master Victor Vasarely, installed in 1969, are one of the visual delights of the city.

On the left, the towering building of the former Soenneken factory; below, the University Library; above, the Kekulé statue in front of the Chemistry Institute; left, the Op Art façade of the Juridikum.

From the Neanderthal man to Adenauer
Bonn Celebrities

When, towards the end of the 70's, a Bonn architect decorated the façade of his house with plaster portraits of famous personalities of bygone and modern times, he provoked some attention, but also some smiles. Since then, the inhabitants of the capital have become 'head-conscious'. Proof of this are the newer, outsized and, at first, somewhat disputed representations of Adenauer before the Chancellery and Beethoven before the concert hall bearing his name.

Bonn's oldest head is a bony original and, like many other things in this city, did not originate from within its walls. The head in question is the skull of Neanderthal man, who lived some 50.000 years ago. Its name indicates the site where it was found — Neanderthal, near Düsseldorf. The remains of the skeleton were discovered there in 1856. The characteristic features of this human species which died out during the last ice age are the low and wide skull vault with a receding forehead and heavy supraorbital ridges. The sturdily-built body was approximately 1.60 metres tall.

The second-oldest Bonn head proves that the area of the present-day capital was already inhabited long before the Romans came, some 2.000 years ago. Remains of Cro-Magnon man, who lived in about 16.000 BC, were found near Oberkassel, and are among the well-preserved treasures of the Rheinisches Landesmuseum.

The gravestone of the first Bonn inhabitant known to us by name, the Roman legionary Publius Claudius, is also preserved in this museum. A copy of the stone stands in the Römerstrasse, on the spot once occupied by the north gate of the old Roman castrum. Publius Claudius, a native of southern France, came to the Rhine with the 1st Legion in c. AD 35. Some five years later he died at the age of 48 after 25 years in the Roman army and shortly before his discharge. This last is concluded by historians from the fact that he is in civilian clothes.

The only Bonn-born member of the teaching corps of the young University was Johann Jakob Noeggerath (1788—1877). In 1821 he became professor of mineralogy and mining, but frequently left his ivory tower and became well-known to a broader public. The seated statue on his tomb shows him gazing critically into the distance. The sculptor, Albert Küppers, whose own last resting place in Poppelsdorf is quite inconspicuous, thus introduced a realistic note into funerary art. One of the first students of the Rheinische Friedrich-Wilhelms University was Karl Simrock (1802—1876), who was expelled from the Prussian civil service for writing a poem in praise of the French July revolution. However, in 1853 he became the first professor of German studies at Bonn University.

Another native son of the city has been sculpted out of stone or marble, bronze or plaster thousands of times, and can be found on countless library shelves and pianos. His portrait was painted eight hundred times, and since 1986 his brooding likeness has been immortalized in the form of a 25-ton colossus made of reinforced concrete. The person in question is the composer Ludwig van Beethoven. For the opening of the 32nd Beethoven festival, this work entitled 'Beethon 86', by the Düsseldorf professor of sculpture Klaus Kammerich, was released from its styrofoam cast, into which it had

been poured several days earlier with the help of a road-construction company.

The sculpture in front of the Beethovenhalle was modelled on the 'Portrait of Ludwig van Beethoven' executed by Joseph Stieler in the 19th century. Kammerich first had a black-and-white photograph taken of it, and set the darker areas in deeply furrowed concrete blocks. Thus the distinctive strong-willed features can be recognized only from certain angles: otherwise it looks like a rugged abstract concrete monument, over three metres in height. When the artist was assembling the moulds made in his studio with a saw of his own construction on the lawn, he guarded the work himself from a Dormobile, in order to prevent iconoclasts from destroying it.

'The Rhine — Germany's river, not Germany's border' is one of the oft-quoted sayings of Ernst Moritz Arndt. It is no wonder

that the people raised a monument to this poet and champion of German unity who courageously wielded his pen against Napoleon, was Baron von Stein's private secretary and rector of the Alma Mater. From his pedestal he watches the Rhine, pointing to the river with one hand. The statue, standing at the Alter Zoll, was first unveiled on July 29, 1865, and on March 22, 1951, was officially unveiled again. In 1818, Arndt, who was born on the island of Rügen, was appointed to the chair of modern history at the newly-founded university in Bonn, where he died in 1860. His house in the Adenauerallee is now a museum.

Although the personality cult is a thorn in the flesh of democracy, there was a general wish to raise a statue of the first Chancellor of the young German republic, Konrad Adenauer. Since 1982, the bronze figure of the 'Old Man' has looked out over the Bundes-

kanzlerplatz. This work by Hubertus von Pilgrim already had its own history before it was put up.

The 'Bundeskanzler Konrad-Adenauer-Haus' Foundation organised a competition for a monument to stand in front of Adenauer's Rhöndorf house. The jury decided on von Pilgrim's entry, but there was strong opposition to the raising of the statue. Finally the memorial was given to the city of Bonn by the Foundation and placed before the former Chancellor's office.

His life is depicted on plaques behind the figure. A rose symbolises the passion for gardening of the 'Old Man from Rhöndorf' as well as the blossoming of the German republic after the war. The cathedral of Reims is a reminder of the reconciliation between France and Germany, the cathedral of Cologne of Adenauer's time as the city's mayor. The Prussian eagle stands for his work as the

chairman of the Prussian State Council, the bound hands for his forced political abstention in the Third Reich. Adenauer is also depicted as Chancellor, speaking in front of the Federal Eagle. Europa and a bull are symbols of Adenauer's humanism and also represent his political aims. An image of the Rhine and the Siebengebirge ('seven hills') points not only to the Chancellor's home, but also to the river as an artery of Europe. Finally, a cross stands for Adenauer's Christian faith.

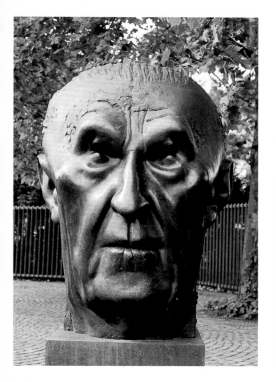

Just as Adenauer and Charles de Gaulle fought for peace in Europe, in the Kaiser's time a woman fought for peace within her own four walls, when the waves of dispute between the members of the Corporations, who had fallen out during the cultural war, threatened to overflow. This was the landlady of the Linden Inn, Anne Schumacher, usually called Ännchen. Her hostelry, much patronized by students, made Bad Godesberg famous far beyond the Rhine valley. Among the Bonn students who often came to celebrate at the foot of the Godesburg, this hard-working and sturdy woman enjoyed great respect and a high reputation.

'Not a drop in the glass', the popular song written by Rudolf Baumbach and set to a melody by Franz Abt, which was included in a book of German drinking songs in 1878, was not actually written with the *Lindenwirtin* (landlady) in view. Two Bonn students later added the last verse about her:

Do you know who the landlady was,
Black of eye and black of hair?
Ännchen, it was, the gentle and fine.
Do you know where the Linde stood
Well-known to every student?
In Godesberg on the Rhine.

The celebrated inn-keeper tried to discourage the song, as she did not consider herself as gentle as it described her. While she had won the fight against poverty after taking over the poor inn and farm from her parents, she lost this battle. With the fall of the Empire in World War I, the good old student drinking days were over, and Ännchen Schumacher retired from business.

The city of Godesberg, in which she died in 1935, made her an honorary citizen. Her tomb is in the Burgfriedhof cemetary.

August Wilhelm von Schlegel (1767—1846), the most famous professor of the young university, is said to have started his lectures after a certain ceremony: first came his servant and placed candles and sugar-water on the desk, then he returned bringing the professor's folder, and only then did the professor himself enter and start his lecture. When on one occasion the students imitated this ritual, the art history and literature professor stared at them stony-faced and started his lecture without more ado.

Above and left page: The monumental Adenauer statue on the Bundeskanzlerplatz; left, the Ernst Moritz Arndt memorial at the Alter Zoll; above the portrait of the *Lindenwirtin* Ännchen Schumacher in Bad Godesberg.

39

Not only the Ninth
Cultur and the Arts

The name of Ludwig van Beethoven is undoubtedly closely connected with the cultural life of the city of Bonn. However, the slogan 'Bonn is more' is certainly justified. Several museums of international repute are located in this university city, commercial theatres supplement the programme offered by the city-subsidized stages, and even the alternative cultural scene has its place in the city's life — and budget.

The Akademisches Kunstmuseum in the Hofgarten (palace gardens) is a real treasure trove of the fine arts. With about 2.000 pieces, it owns the largest collection of casts of antique sculpture in Germany. The important collection of original Greek and Roman exhibits — vases and terracotta, bronze and marble objects — is also not to be missed. The building itself was constructed in 1824 according to the plans of Waesemann, revised by Schinkel, as an anatomy school. But as early as 1884 it was used to house the antiquities collection, admired even by Goethe. The main feature of the building is the rotunda of the 'Theatrum Anatomicum'.

The Alexander Koenig Museum in the Adenauerallee has a reputation both as a research centre and as a zoological museum. Alexander Koenig, whose father had amassed a fortune from sugar-beet plantations in Russia, had the museum built in neo-Renaissance style between 1912 and 1914. He bequeathed his own collections, gathered during his travels, to the German state in 1929. The museum was opened in 1934. It houses an important ornithological

collection of 80.000 exhibits and the largest collection of East-Asian butterflies in the world. While the scientific collections are open only to specialists, the public stand amazed in front of the dioramas showing the animals in their natural surroundings.

The Bonn Opera, the 'Scala on the Rhine', is clearly visible on the city skyline. The concrete building, constructed between 1962 and 1965 according to plans by Klaus Gessler and W. Berg-Erlag, is faced with scale-like metal plaques. The complex with terraces and balconies faces onto the river. The city theatre and ballet are also based here. With government support, it has been possible to bring many world-famous artists to the Rhine. Here they all perform on culture-laden soil, so to speak — during the construction of the theatre garage in 1982, remains of Roman and Celtic settlements were discovered.

Drama, music and dance in the streets of the city as well are the backbone of the 'Bonn Summer', a programme of artistic and cultural events that has won itself an international reputation, not least because folklore groups from all over the world form a regular attraction. Rock music concerts are held frequently on the great lawns of the Rheinaue park. The city streets also offer a number of greater and lesser works by renowned artists of various styles and epochs. In front of the Town Hall stands the 20-metre-tall 'Chronos 15', weighing ten tons, a sculpture by Nicho-

Above and right-hand page, far right, the Akademisches Kunstmuseum; right and below, the Museum Alexander König.

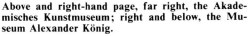

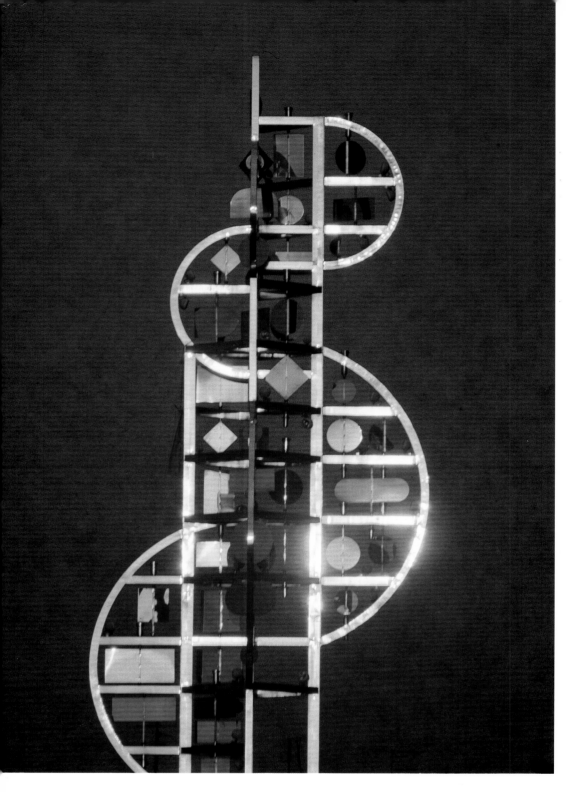

las Schöffer who lives in Paris. He worked on the figure for two years, with the help of an engineer and a computer. Originally, 57 metal mirrors, powered by concealed engines, reflected the sunlight by day, and the beams of 57 spotlights at night. However, the complicated technology did not stand up to the Bonn climate, and the engines and lamps were subsequently removed with the artist's permission. Moved by the wind, the mirrors now reflect the sunlight by day and the light of three lamps by night.

An important collection of German painting and sculpture is housed in the city Museum of Art. It is based on the foundation of Dr. Franz Obernier, who in 1882 bequeathed to the city his collection of 19th-century art of the Düsseldorf school. The work of expressionist August Macke (1887—1914) is one of the highlights of the collection today. Macke lived in Bonn from 1910, and in 1913 helped promote the new movement by the 'Exhibition of Rhine Expressionists'.

The Rheinisches Landesmuseum was founded in 1820. After the destruction of the old building in 1893, it was moved to a renovated house in 1909 and to a new building in 1967. The extensive collections give an overview of the Rhine area's cultural history from the Stone Age to the present day. Changing exhibitions of contemporary art provide interesting counterpoints. An external proof that not only 'ancient rubble' is exhibited in the museum is Norbert Krickel's plastic art, 'Kräftebündel', placed in front of the main entrance. Important exhibits from prehistoric times include the skull of Neanderthal man, and from the Roman era — the Caelius Stone, the only evidence of the battle of the Teutoburger Wald. Ulrich Ruck-

Above, the light-statue 'Chronos 15' at the Town Hall; above right, the Opera, called the 'Scala on the Rhine'; below, street theatre at the Münsterplatz and a rock concert in the Rheinaue park.

riem's 'Stein zum 10. Oktober 1981', in front of the façade facing the Bachstrasse, brings us right up to date. This monument, made of dolomite blocks, commemorates a great peace demonstration in which 300.000 people took part.

All year round, cultural pilgrims from all over the world visit the Beethoven house in the Bonngasse and linger reverently before a bust of the most-performed composer in the world, in the modest attic room at the back of the house. This is where Ludwig van Beethoven was born on December 16, 1770. His father, a court tenor, and mother, Maria Magdalena, lived in poor conditions in the back part of the imposing house. In 1889, twelve Bonn citizens acquired the run-down house and arranged the museum with numerous handwritten documents, portraits and illustrations, statues and instruments. More important for scholarly research are the Beethoven archives in the house next door. These contain photocopies of almost everything the composer ever wrote — letters, scores, etc. — and a library with 3,700 books and 700 records.

The Beethoven memorial by Ernst Julius Hähnel on the Münsterplatz was raised in 1845, to mark the 75th anniversary of his birth. An association was formed to collect and administer the funds for the statue. The composer Franz Liszt gave the last 10,000 taler that were needed. The ceremonial unveiling of the statue, which also inaugurated the first Beethoven festival, was witnessed from the balcony of the present-day Post Office, by Queen Victoria of Great Britain and King Frederick William IV of Prussia. When the cloth dropped from the statue, the crowned heads found themselves staring straight at the composer's back. Surprised, the king exclaimed: "Hey, he has his back turned to us!" Alexander von Humboldt, who was also present, saved the situation by quipping: "Yes, even in life he was always an ill-mannered fellow."

Today the bronze maestro has to suffer the ill-manners of those around him: demonstrators press red flags into his hands, punks die his hair and the ubiquitous pigeons do their worst.

The Grazien-Brunnen (Three Graces' Foun-

tain) at the Dreieck is a symbiosis of old and new art. On the basin of the old fountain stand the Three Graces by the contemporary artist Ernemann Sander. In the Poppelsdorfer Allee there used to be a fountain with the figure of a maiden, popularly called the 'Bonn herring-girl', holding a fish from which the water flowed. During the building of the subway, when the fountain was taken apart, this figure was lost. Only the basin remained, and this was returned to its original position in 1976.

It is not only the Beethoven festival and the great performances that make the city of Bonn interesting for lovers of the arts. Almost daily, new exhibitions of the various federal states' missions and agencies mirror cultural trends throughout the country and the world. The Prussian Cultural Heritage Foundation in the Wissenschaftszentrum in the Kennedyallee puts on exhibitions which provide a spiritual link with Berlin. Contemporary Bonn artists exhibit in the building beside La Redoute, the former electoral prince's theatre, and in the former electoral gardener's house in the Baumschulallee.

Two exceptional establishments from the cultural point of view are the only Women's Museum in the Federal Republic of Germany, at No. 10 Krausfeld, in the Nordstadt, and the Duisdorf Theater im Keller (Cellar Theatre), called 'TIK' for short, which proclaims itself the only amateur theatre with a permanent home. Its actors are participants in adult education centre courses who here put into practice, through cabaret and detective-story plays, the theory learnt during classes.

On the left-hand page, the Grazien-Brunnen; above, the Rheinisches Landesmuseum with the 'Kräftebündel' statue; above right, the Beethoven memorial; right, the entrance to the Beethoven house.

The People, the Market and the Münster
The Inner City

For centuries the two centres of the old city, the Marktplatz, in front of the residence of the secular authorities, and the Münsterplatz, in front of the seat of spiritual power, have been meeting places of the citizens. The whole of the inner city is now a great pedestrian zone which throngs with life from early morning till late at night. Yet people find time to take a break, sit in the cool shadowy church if they are in need of spiritual peace, or on the sunny terrace of some café if they feel like a chat. Others, again, prefer to loiter at Beethoven's feet or at the market fountain for an exchange of small-talk.

The Marktfontäne (market fountain) is actually a memorial to Electoral Prince Max Frederick, who personally laid the cornerstone for it on June 30, 1777. For two years a symbol of the electoral princes topped the obelisk, but was lost in 1798, during the turmoils of that year. The coats-of-arms on the shaft of the memorial also fell victim to the Revolution. During the last renovation, the tradition-conscious restorers wanted to top the memorial again, but the republican spirit was strongly opposed to this and the idea was dropped.

Above, a view of the city, with the Münster and 'Lange Eugen' building, up to the Siebengebirge; right, the Marktplatz with the obelisk and Sternstrasse; right-hand page, the chestnut-lined avenue running from the Poppelsdorf palace to the university.

From the Münster, beyond the Beethoven monument, the main post office (the former Palais Radermacher) can be seen. A relief on the gable depicts the blessing of the mail. The banks and shops around the Münsterplatz have been restored so as to preserve a harmonious unity of both form and colour. Two great but quite different thoroughfares cut the centre of the city into four equally diverse parts: the line of the old Römerstrasse running north-south, and the Baroque axis in the east-west direction. Whereas the former, passing through the government and diplomatic areas, is the main traffic artery and barely allows pedestrians a passage, the latter is more reminiscent of leisurely times when horse-drawn carriages were the only traffic hazard. It stretches like a ribbon from the Rhine via the Town Hall to the Poppelsdorfer Allee, and further to the Baroque church on the Kreuzberg. Mostly reserved for pedestrians,

Above, view from the Kaiserplatz over the Poppelsdorf palace to the Baroque Kreuzberg church; right, the Botanical Gardens; on the right-hand page, the Beethoven memorial in front of the Post Office; below, the Münsterplatz.
On the following page, the east apse of the Münster flanked by two towers.

the 'Pop-Allee' gives a clear picture of the 18th-century city lay-out. The Poppelsdorfer Allee, crossed by railway tracks but made passable for pedestrians by a subway, was originally planned as a canal in the 18th century, but subsequently laid out as a chestnut-lined avenue. Whoever goes to the Kaiserplatz, a favourite meeting place of young and old alike, can still enjoy the view which the electors and their architects created.

The history of the Münster was always closely bound up with the fate of the city. Several phases of construction link the Early

Christian memorial to the city's patron saints, Cassius and Florentius, to the present-day basilica. The massive but slender-looking crossing tower, 92 metres high and visible from afar, is one of its outstanding features. The 11th-century east apse with its two tall flanking towers ranks among the major early mediaeval architectural works. During the Calogne religious war, the mediaeval interior decoration of the cathedral was almost completely lost: today the interior is predominantly Baroque in style. The four stone sarcophagi in the crypt are

thought to be martyrs' graves. Inside the cathedral the first thing that catches the eye is the large bronze statue of St. Helena, honoured as the founder of the first church raised on this site. As with the elevations, a closer inspection of the interior reveals traces of the Gothic style, which began to exert an influence on the Romanesque architecture while the construction of the cathedral was in progress.

Also worthy of note is the Romanesque cloister, on the south side of the cathedral, of which only three sides were preserved

Above, the interior of the Münster with the bronze statue of St. Helena; above right, the massive crossing tower and the two towers flanking the east apse, below the Beethoven memorial; below, the cloister, and oasis of peace in the heart of the bustling city.

after the rebuilding of the nave. The capitals of the columns have a diversity of ornamentation. Stepping into the cloister from the bustling Münsterplatz one feels transported to another age and an oasis of peace.

The parish church of St. Martin stood on the Martinsplatz, in front of the east apse of the

Münster, from 1140 until 1812. Its foundations are marked by reddish basalt stones.

Since the Middle Ages, the Remigiusstrasse has linked the Münster and the busy market. In the Marktplatz the visitor can experience the mundane life of Bonn when, towards closing time, the stall-holders start to extoll their goods in a strong Rhineland accent and engage in a usually not very serious 'price war'. In winter the lamps are turned on in the afternoon and bathe the scene in a pleasant warm glow. Street musicians try to attract the attentions and coins of passersby: sometimes it is an old barrel-organ player, sometimes South American musicians who enchant the listeners with the magic of Andean flutes, drums and guitars. A corner further on, high-school or university students may be trying to make some extra pocket-money with nostalgic songs of the Sixties.

The Sternstrasse, curving away from the market square, is one of the few inner-city streets to have been spared the wartime destruction. Its narrow gabled houses still convey the atmosphere of the Middle Ages, when they were built as merchants' and craftsmen's dwellings. Destiny has given the Sternstrasse a special role — to link the old Town Hall and the new one.

Above left, the Sternstrasse, a reminder of the Middle Ages; below, a pre-Christmas market scene and the Remigiusstrasse between the Münster and the Marktplatz; above, the Südstadt quarter, crisscrossed by avenues; below, a barrel-organ player.

57

In the evenings, when the shops close, the city becomes gradually emptier and quiter. This is when the first 'night birds' mingle with the last of the housewives, shopkeepers and office-workers, laden with heavy shopping bags or briefcases, who are going home to spend a relaxing evening.

Peaceful avenues like those in the Südstadt quarter give a sense of security and permanence. The visitor should stroll through this area slowly, gazing upwards, in order to observe its treasures, or even wait for winter to see the façades in their full glory — and realise that not everything here is a façade. Towards the end of the last century, Bonn's Südstadt, like the villa quarter in Bad Godesberg, was the favourite residential area of industrialists and academics, archi-

One the left-hand page, the old Town Hall; above, the modern Town Hall.

tects and building constructors. This is where the educated middle class congregated, and where an epoch ended.

The fact that the war had spared this quarter was long regarded as a disadvantage. Altered façades and modernised windows, even demolitions and the erection of intrusive new buildings, scarred it. Thanks to a change in attitude, however, supported by façade competitions, the old house-fronts are now resplendent with their former beauty. The buildings were renovated inside as well, providing them with all modern con-

19th-century façades in Bonn's Südstadt convey an old-world atmosphere and make walks here a pleasure in all seasons.

veniences. But even in those postwar times the streets and houses were never moribund. The large number of cafés, inns and shops were proof that people still lived there — elderly women left over from the good old days, students, guest workers and a certain kind of bohemian who managed to find a place here.

In the middle of the 19th century, when Bonn started to spread southwards, the city architect Paul Thomann put forward the excellent idea of making an urban plan for the area between the Poppelsdorfer Allee, the Reuterstrasse, the Rhine and the Hofgarten (palace garden). However, the indi-

vidual interests of private landowners were too strong, and the Südstadt grew up without any overall plan. The unity of the area today is therefore all the more surprising. It is seen not only in the style of the façades, but also in the very disciplined block development, with much greenery in the inner courtyards and along the streets.

A decisive role in the 'rediscovery' of the Südstadt in the 70's and 80's was played by a handful of gallery-owners who appreciated Bonn's artistic value and particularly admired the atmosphere of this part of the city. They were followed into the area by a whole series of other businesses catering to

Left, the modern Kaiserpassage shopping precinct; above, the coat-of-arms of the Bonnsch brewery.

cultivated tastes: wine and delicatessen stores, boutiques and fashionable taverns and restaurants. However, some of the old student pubs and the 'Kerze artists' cellar still flourish alongside these.

The new admiration for the old decor brought a partial change in the type of resident: more prosperous citizens came back, buying and renovating the houses. The Südstadt is now a jewel of the city once more. Old stepped gables, lattice windows and stucco decoration have all been lovingly restored. Other buildings from the turn of the century have also been renovated and maintained. On the fairly rare occasions when snow blankets everything, this quarter has the charm and feeling of permanance of the old-fashioned Christmas-card scene.

Numerous meeting places of various kinds offer a homely and pleasant atmosphere. Catholic students and the Italian community have found a 'home' in the Namen-Jesu-Kirche (church of the Name of Jesus) in the Bonngasse. Begun in 1689 and consecrated in 1717, this is an important work of 'Jesuit Gothic', an architectural style which draws mostly on Gothic forms. The two-aisled nave is decorated in blue, gold and white, giving it a festive character. On the outside, it stands out from the surrounding buildings by its two towers.

The attractive arcades and halls of the new Kaiserpassage, with its shops and cafés, lying between the Münster and the Kaiserplatz, are a good example of how old and new can be pleasingly combined. Here one can enjoy a leisurely stroll even during the frequent rain.

Where there is so much communal life, there must be a brewery. Bonn has two, in fact. Although the electoral princes preferred Pils and Kölsch (a strong lager from Cologne), the city has long had its own type of beer: Bonnsch. The master brewer in the little brewery at the Sterntor still produces this top fermented, naturally cloudy beverage, which is highly recommended when taken in moderate quantities. The master brewer can be observed at work from the visitors' room in this brewery.

The business life of Bonn, is not, of course, confined to gastronomy. Even though almost every fourth citizen of the capital is a federal or municipal civil servant or some other administrative employee, and though there are large numbers of 'unproductive' lobbyists standing around at the listening posts or informing deputies of the views of their interest groups, considerable industry is to be found on the city outskirts. Hence the popular sticker put out by the city's press and advertising association, which shows lips pursed for a kiss and bears the slogan 'Made in Bonn'. The favourite product of the capital is probably the *Gummibärchen* — the jelly-bear. Truckloads of sweets and liquorice leave the loading-bays every day, to bring pleasure to children and adults alike.

A large company in Mehlem produces pantographs for the high-speed French TGV train. Roofing felt is produced in Beuel, as are decorations and badges, very popular during the carnival. A renowned firm makes organs for churches and concert halls, while the flag factory is capable of satisfying the capital's requirements for such decorations. Varnish and egg liqueur, containers and packaging, refrigerators and electronic elements, leave the city daily. The Rheinhafen (harbour) on the northern city limits is becoming increasingly important in this process.

A peaceful spot not far from the busy ringroad is the Alter Friedhof (old cemetery) on the Bornheimer Strasse. Joseph Clement had it arranged in 1715 as a burial place for soldiers and strangers. When the parish graveyards became full up and were closed in 1787, it became the main cemetery. Although it was extended several times during the 19th century, in 1884 it, too, had to be closed. Today only those with old family tombs have a chance of being laid to rest here. The Alter Friedhof with its numerous monuments is a guide through Bonn's cultural history. This is where Beethoven's mother, Maria Magdalena, was buried — her grave was rediscovered only in 1932. Clara and Robert Schumann, the writers Liese and Wilhelm Schmidtbonn, and Adele Schopenhauer, sister of the philosopher, are among those interred here.

The Kreuzkirche (church of the Cross) on the continuation of the axis that runs from the University to the Poppelsdorf palace, stands on a hill and is visible from afar. As early as the 15th century, pilgrims climbed the Kreuzberg (hill of the Cross) by four different paths in order to pray at the sacred Cross. Today this traditional place of pilgrimage has become a popular church for young couples to marry in. The church was built in 1627—28, according to the plans of Christof Wamser, architect of the Jesuit church of Cologne, by Archbishop Ferdinand, who brought Servite monks to the monastery here. From 1855 until 1872, it was the home of Jesuits, and from 1889 to 1961 it housed Franciscans. Today it is a school for Third World students.

The cruciform hall church owes its Baroque additions to the Elector Clement Augustus, who had the chancel built and the 'holy steps' constructed between 1746 and 1757. The three flights of marble steps, designed by Balthasar Neumann, were inspired by the *scala sancta* in Rome and have parallels in Austria and Bohemia. The central flight of 28 steps, sanctified by parts of the Cross and holy relics, can be ascended only on the knees and without weapons. They lead to a chapel with a Crucifixion group. This addition to the church is also called 'The House of Pilate', because of the group of figures above the central portal, depicting Pontius Pilate and a soldier presenting Christ to the people *(Ecce Homo)*. The high altar of the church, also by Balthasar Neumann, was

Above, the interior and exterior of the Baroque Kreuzberg church; right, the Alte Friedhof cemetery with the grave of Clara and Robert Schumann.

donated in 1747 by Clement Augustus, as was the richly ornamented pulpit.

Though the climate in the lowland bay of Cologne may not always be ideal, the nearby Kottenforst gives the inhabitants of the Rhine valley a chance to breathe in clear upland air. A network of paths and avenues, totalling 55 kilometres in length, criss-cross this nature reserve of some 100 square kilometres, which stretches far beyond the Bonn city limits. Two thirds of the Kottenforst comprise deciduous trees, including some gigantic beeches. An open-air enclo-

sure with fallow deer and wild boar at Waldau, the Hunting Lodge, once a changing post for horses and dogs, and the Kottenforst railway station are attractive features of the area.

The great forest was a royal estate in Frankish times, but was given to the archbishopric of Cologne by Emperor Otto I in 973. Under the electoral princes, between 1727 and 1756 the forest was laid out for hunting. Numerous paths were traced and had to be consolidated because of the marshy land. The palatial Herzogsfreude hunting lodge at Röttgen used to be the centre of the hunting area. From this little castle, which has not been preserved, the paths spread out radially. During the sticky summer heat, certain parts of Bonn can thank these historic 'aisles' for the flow of fresher air.

Even more popular than the Kottenforst is the Rheinaue leisure park. This land, stretching from the 'Lange Eugen' in the north to the American colony near Plittersdorf in the south, offers some 350 acres of open countryside. In 1979, 250 acres of this were used for the Federal Garden Show. Over several years the flat arable land was transformed by gardeners into a hilly park with intersecting paths, large lawns, barbecue places and 1.5-kilometre-long lake with many coves. 38 nations took part in the garden show and 7.6 million visitors came from near and far to see the flower festival, which lasted 178 days.

A Japanese garden, a stone Beethoven sculpture, a 'classical' path with copies of 26 Roman statues from the Landesmuseum, and a playground for children are reminders of the garden show. Although its high cost led to some heated arguments at the time, today both critics and supporters of the garden show use the area equally. It is not only a family excursion place: on some summer week-ends great crowds are attracted by the flea-market held here. The city authorities also organise many festivities here, such as the traditional 'Rhine in Flames', when Beethoven's music is performed in perfect harmony with a great display of pyrotechnics.

The bank of the Rhine is very popular with walkers, hikers and cyclists. From the state border of Rheinland-Palatinate in the south to the city limits at the harbour of Graurheindorf in the north, the left bank of the river, in particular, offers an impressive panorama, marred only by the cement factory in

southern Beuel and its concrete loading bays.

From the Siebengebirge to the mouth of the Sieg on the right bank of the Rhine there are many restaurants and inns, some of which have a historic past and impressive guest-lists. Romantic terraces invite the weary to rest with a glass of wine. The tow-path along the bank is a reminder of the times when horses used to draw ships up the Rhine. As the horses always looked towards the river out of the corner of their eyes, the inhabitants of the left bank call the opposite side of the Rhine the 'Schäl Sick', the squinting side.

A large number of clubs and associations offer Bonn's inhabitants a wide choice of activities in the cultural and sports fields. Free initiative is also active, and new, international amusements have become popular alongside the traditional ones. Thus the French national game of *boules* has in the meantime become a common sight in Bonn's parks.

The Federal Garden Show in 1979 left the inhabitants of Bonn with the Rheinaupark, a favourite leisure area not far from the government district. Flea-markets, fairs and the 'Rhine in Flames' event are held here as well.

Rail, Road and River
Communications

Whoever enters the main railway station of Bonn can hardly get on the wrong platform, a local joke goes, since there are only two. This is not quite true. The over 100-year-old sandstone station has four platforms, with trains going in three directions: north, south and west, although this last is only a slow local train to the Voreifel.

When the railway between Bonn and Cologne was opened in 1844, this offered a no less leisurely and picturesque trip. However, today it is the busiest line in Germany, with about 300 trains a day. No wonder that many Bonn citizens complain of spending half their lives waiting before closed ramps. A number of subways makes things easier for pedestrians, but motorists must have patience. The expansion of the number of railway tracks has often been discussed, but this idea has never been translated into action. Meanwhile, the Bonn city fathers are worried that they may lose the Intercity connection, since the Federal Railways are toying with the idea of relieving the Cologne-Frankfurt stretch by building a new high-speed line bypassing Bonn. Less important is the railway line with a little station in Beuel which winds south between vineyards and the Rhine.

On the other hand, the capital is in no danger of losing its 'White Fleet' on the Rhine. Not only the boats of the regional passenger line stand at the landing stages at Brassertufer and the Godesberg bastion: the Cologne-Düsseldorf fleet also anchors here. Those who enjoy pleasant river cruises, made even pleasanter by good service and the panorama of the romantic Rhine valley, have come to the right place. They must, however, also have time.

For the people on either side of the river, it was for centuries a border which could only be crossed by little ferry-boats. There is still a passenger ferry between Bonn and Beuel, while car ferries connect Bad Godesberg and Niederdollendorf, Mehlem and Königswinter.

In 1898 the first Rhine bridge between Bonn and Beuel was built on the site of today's Kennedy bridge. Its construction provoked a quarrel between the two towns about the financing of the construction, as Beuel refused to participate. The Bonn inhabitants got their own back by raising the 'Brückenmännchen' (bridge manikin), a stone figure turning its backside to the other bank of the Rhine. There was a 'turn about' in affairs after the rebuilding of the bridge, blown up during World War II by retreating German troops. The 'Brückenmännchen', hanging from a pier, had its behind turned towards Frankfurt, the unsuccessful candidate for the federal capital. Today, the figure

The Kennedy bridge is a pulsing artery for motor vehicles and trains between Bonn and Beuel, while the 'White Fleet' on the River gives promise of pleasure and romance.

68

faces in its original direction on the western bridgehead.

From 1902, the 'electric' crossed the completed bridge between the railway stations on either side of the Rhine. As early as 1893 the Bonn-Bad Godesberg-Mehlem steam railways had started operation, and in 1929 this stretch was also electrified. A steam train drawn by a puffing, smoking, steel horse, popularly called 'Fiery Elijah', ran westward to the Vorgebirge. Today, modern suburban railway trains cross the Kennedy bridge and connect Bonn and Bad Godesberg, running partly underground through the city.

Although the web of motorways in and around Bonn is criticised by nature conservationists, the first stretch of German Autobahn, between Bonn and Cologne, completed in 1932, is now itself classified as a monument worthy of preservation. In connection with the construction of highways in the Seventies, two more bridges were built: the Friedrich-Ebert bridge in the north of the city, also called the 'harp' because of its elegant construction, and the Konrad-Adenauer bridge (south bridge), between Ramersdorf and the federal government quarter.

Above and right, passenger vessels of the 'White Fleet' on the Rhine; right, the 'Brückenmännchen' at the western bridgehead; below, the Rhine panorama seen from the east bank; on the right-hand page, above, the Friedrich-Ebert bridge.

Churches, Nature and Carnival
Visiting Beuel

The Kennedy bridge connects the inner city of Bonn with the part on the right bank of the Rhine, the city district of Beuel. Between the mouth of the Sieg in the north and the Siebengebirge in the south lie the quarters of Schwarzrheindorf, Vilich-Rheindorf, Vilich and Geisler in the north, and Limperich, Kündinghoven and Ramersdorf in the south. To the east are Vilich-Müldorf, Pützchen Holzlar and the Siegburg nature park, to which the forested hill of Ennert also belongs. Oberkassel, Hoholz and Holzlar were separate villages until 1969. Although Vilich was originally the more important place, in time the growth of industry and population gave Beuel greater weight. The former Town Hall, a rectangular modern building, today houses the district government. One room is dedicated to Beuel's twin town, Stolp in Pomerania. Nearby is the late-Gothic brick St. Josephskirche, where organ recitals are regularly given, which has a carillon of 62 bells.

Quite close to the southern bridgehead stands the Mehlemsche Haus, a late-Baroque building which now houses the city music school. An enthroned Caesar, dating from the 19th century, watches over the garden entrance. Until 1945 it stood at the

Rheinbrücke, since it was believed that Caesar had raised the first bridge over the Rhine at that spot. While this theory no longer "holds water", it has been proved that the Romans had a settlement at Beuel in order to control the ferry crossing to Bonn. Although the whole region is predominantly Catholic, there is room for other confessions and religions. Beuel, for instance, is the seat of the Greek Orthodox Church in Germany. The metropolitan church in the Dietrich-Bonhoeffer-Strasse was consecrated in 1979. In accordance with the Greek Church tradition, in 1983 it was decorated with wall paintings, the most impressive of which is the representation of Christ in the dome.

The first abbess of Vilich abbey, Adelheid, who was born in 970 in Geldern and died in Cologne in 1015, had been revered as a saint for centuries before the Vatican officially canonised her in 1966. Her parents, the feudal lord Megingoz and his wife Geberga, were the founders of the abbey. According to tradition, Adelheid caused a stream to flow when she struck the ground with her staff during a time of great drought and hardship. Pilgrims started flocking to this

Above, the Greek Orthodox metropolitan church; below, the Adelheid spring at Pützchen and the Mehlemsches Haus at the Beueler Brückenkopf; rihgt, the dome of the Greek Orthodox Church.

spring, in present-day Pützchen, since its water was supposed to have curative properties, especially for eye troubles. The spring was built up and a stone cross raised. The "Pützchens Markt" developed with the arrival of the pilgrims.

The pilgrims' path also led to the abbey of Vilich itself, whose church was enlarged on several occasions. The members of the Order of St. Augustine who live in the abbey building, dating from 1624, are dedicated to caring for the elderly. Also in the Vilich area is the privately-owned Lede castle, approached along an avenue of poplar trees. The moats and park have been preserved. The castle was originally built of rough-hewn stone and basalt in the 14th century on earlier foundations. After its destruction in 1583 during the religious war of Cologne, it was left in ruins until the beginning of the 20th century, when it was rebuilt.

Right-bank Bonn is set in beautiful natural surroundings, making it a very popular re-creation area. The Siegaue, with its long walks and bicycle paths, is a favourite excursion place. This ecologically valuable area has been proclaimed a bird reservation: the many waterways and abundance of insects and snails provide marsh and river birds with ideal nesting conditions. Many families enjoy a Sunday ride there on the old ferry, while motorists have been provided with a bridge spanning the high-water area. The

1200 acres of Ennert forest are also mostly a nature reserve. Paths lead through the romantic wilderness of lakes and precipices created by the quarrying of stone. The Dorn-heckensee lake has become a very popular resort of naturists, much to the chagrin of nature-watchers.

At the motorway junction called the Ramers-dorfer Knoten (Ramersdorf knot) lies the Ramersdorf Deutschordenskommende, a seat of the Teutonic Order, first mentioned in records in 1254 and sold when the Order was secularised in 1809. The Romanesque chapel built by the Order in 1230 was taken down stone by stone and re-erected in the Alter Friedhof in Bonn. A fire in 1882 badly damaged the remaining buildings. The Baron von Oppenheim rebuilt the Kom-mende as a manor in 1884. Since the last renovation, in the 1980's the building has housed a hotel, an antique shop and the castle museum. The beautiful park that once surrounded the Ramersdorf Kommende has mostly been destroyed by road-building.

Oberkassel is known to scholars for the finds of Stone Age human remains: in 1914, the skulls of a man and woman, the so-called Oberkassel people, were discovered here. They lived some 16,000 years BC and belonged to the Cro-Magnon type. Ober-kassel is also the birth place of the writer and freedom-fighter Gottfried Kinkel (1815—1882). A bust opposite the Prince of

Lippe's country house in the Hauptstrasse commemorates this professor of art history and publisher of the *Bonner Zeitung,* who together with his wife, Johanna, founded the 'Maikäferbund' writers' association. He was sentenced to life imprisonment for his part in the Baden insurrection in 1849, but with the help of his friend Carl Schurz managed to escape the following year to England, where he lectured at Hyde Park College and elsewhere. From 1866 until his death in 1882, he was a professor of archaeology and art history in Zurich.

The parish church in Schwarzrheindorf, one of the jewels of Romanesque architecture in the Rhineland, is noted for its unusual two-storied structure and its mural decoration. Count Arnold von Wied had the church built with a Greek-cross ground-plan, without a nave, as his burial place near his castle. In 1151, soon after he was elected arch-bishop of Cologne, he dedicated the church to St. Clement in the presence of the Emperor Conrad III and numerous other exalted guests. Through an octagonal opening over the crossing of the lower church, the archbishop could follow from his throne in

the upper church the service which was celebrated in front of the altar of the lower one, without being seen by the people below. This construction is reminiscent of Charlemagne's Palatine Chapel in Aachen. After the death of the founder in 1156, his sister Hedwig, an abbess in Essen, had a tower storey and nave added to the church when she founded a Benedictine abbey here. The black robes of the Benedictine Order gave Schwarzrheindorf its name (*schwarz=* black), as opposed to Graurheindorf on the other side of the river, where the grey-clad Cistercian nuns lived.

The most important cycle of Romanesque wall paintings in the Rhineland was uncovered in the lower church between 1854 and 1865. The murals on the vaulting, based on the visions of the Prophet Ezekiel, had been whitewashed over some time during the 17th century, and were not discovered until 1846, when work began on the restoration of the church, which under French rule had served as a stable and store. These wall paintings were executed shortly after the raising of St. Clement's. The paintings in the

The two-storey church of Schwarzrheindorf is one of the most unusual Romanesque churches of the Rhineland. Above right and left, the tower; left, a view through the colonnade; above, statue of the Madonna in the upper church; on the right-hand page, below, the wall paintings of the lower church.

upper church, dating from 1170, were only discovered during restoration work in 1868 and were restored in 1875. They depict Christ as the Judge of the World, the founder Arnold von Wied and his sister Hedwig, and ten saints. The vaulting of the choir has frescoes of the Lamb of God surrounded by the chosen.

The church's position, on top of a little hill in the midst of otherwise flat countryside, and its colourful elevations make it clearly visible from afar. The painting of the façade, carried out in 1974, follows that of well-preserved Gothic church models. From the outer colonnade, there is a magnificent view along the Rhine to the north, as far as Siegburg in the east, the Siebengebirge in the south and the Voreifel in the west.

In olden times the inhabitants of the Beuel region made their living by fishing, a little wine-growing, washing laundry and bleaching cloth. Despite the hard work, they found time to celebrate all the feasts. This fact is commemorated by the Waschweiber Denkmal (washerwomen memorial), the counterpart of the Bonn Brückenmännchen (bridge manikin). It recalls the Weiberfastnacht, the day during the carnival when women take

Above, left, "Pützchens Markt" a popular fair with such attractions as "the largest transportable big wheel in the world"; left, the Beuel "Waschweiber" and fancifully dressed carnival fools; above, Bonn's mayor, Hans Daniels, and Minister Norbert Blüm on the balcony of Beuel Town Hall during the washer-princess's assumption of power on the carnival Thursday.

control, which is celebrated on the right bank of the Rhine with great gusto. Instead of a carnival prince, Beuel has a carnival washer-princess who takes over the sceptre from the Thursday before the carnival until Ash Wednesday. Limperich, Kündighoven and Ramersdorf join together to elect their "LIKURA", who usurps the power of every other authority, and issues joke laws to ensure good cheer and merriment.

The clowning during the carnival was often unpopular with the authorities, who feared real attacks by completely masked persons. The ban on masks and disguises designed to discourage acts of violence during demonstrations is not a modern "invention": the electoral princes in their day enforced such bans in Bonn in times of unrest.

The Castle and Half-Timber
Visiting Bad Godesberg

The garden city of Bad Godesberg extends along the left bank of the Rhine, opposite the Siebengebirge ('seven hills'). Its name comes from 'Wuodenesberg', a place of worship of the Germanic Franks on what is now called Burgberg (castle hill). The name indicates allegiance to the god Woden, who was worshipped on many hilltops. After the conversion of the Franks to Christianity, the heathen cult-place became a shrine of the Archangel Michael, to whom the castle chapel is still dedicated.

At the foot of the hill lies the well-restored old town with the Theaterplatz, the Studio Theatre and the famous inn of the Lindenwirtin Ännchen. The present hostelry is a new building modelled on the old tavern. The ancient Romans, who founded a settlement at the foot of the mountain, appreciated the Godesberg mineral water, which earned the town the name 'Bad'.

In the Middle Ages, the archbishopric of Cologne owned numerous farmsteads in these villages which it was concerned to secure since they brought in a good income. This became even more necessary in 1205 when King Philip built Landskron castle near Remagen as an important stronghold against the archbishopric. In response, in 1210 Archbishop Dietrich I started building a castle on the 60-metre-high basalt peak of the Godesberg. This was greatly enlarged in the time of Konrad von Hochstaden, who also raised the city walls of Bonn and founded Cologne cathedral. For 250 years, the castle was the favourite seat of the Cologne archbishops, who felt safe here even in the most troubled times.

This seemingly impregnable fortress was occupied by the troops of the deposed Archbishop Gebhard Truchsess von Waldburg, who had turned Calvinist. They withstood a four-week siege by the forces of the newly-elected Archbishop Ernest of Bavaria. His brother, Duke Ferdinand of Bavaria, who commanded the army which was to return Cologne to the Catholic faith, placed 1500 pounds of gunpowder under the castle walls and blew a breach in them, but even this was not enough. It was not until 50 soldiers managed to sneak into the castle unobserved and attack the defenders from the rear that the stronghold was finally captured and destroyed, in 1583.

The ruins of the castle became a popular subject among artists of the Romantic period. In 1891 Emperor William II presented it to the commune of Godesberg, which in 1895-96 opened a restaurant there as a further attraction for visitors to the 32-metre-high keep, a popular vantage point for viewing the surrounding area. The reconstruction work for the present hotel and re-

Around the basalt peak with the Bergfried (keep) of Godesburg castle are grouped the Godesberg old town and the villages which became linked up during the postwar building boom. Following pages: The façade of the Ännchen-Center, the Godesburg tower and Zur Lindenwirtin Inn.

staurant, carried out in 1959 according to the plans of architect Gottfried Böhm, created a notably successful blend of the mediaeval and the modern. Böhm also drew up the plans for the red clinker building of the Altstadt-center in the area of the old town.

West of the road leading to the castle hotel lies the Burgfriedhof (castle cemetery). The earthly remains of famous Godesberg personalities, among them Ännchen Schumacher and the famous actor Paul Kemp, rest here on several terraces. In the late 19th and early 20th centuries, upper-class citizens raised a number of costly funerary monuments here, most notably the Jugendstil 'Mother Earth' tomb, depicting the various ages of human life, from the cradle to the grave.

The town of Godesberg was far less important in the past than the castle itself; even Electoral Prince Clement Augustus's attempt to build a health resort around the mineral spring changed little. It was not until about 1790, when the somewhat sickly Archbishop Max Ernest had the so-called 'Draitschbrunnen' spring developed, large parks laid out, and bathing and social facilities raised that things really got going. The most impressive edifice from this period is La Redoute, a rococo mansion started in 1791 according to plans by the court architect Michael Leydel and completed by his son, Adam Franz Friedrich Leydel, in 1830. The electoral prince gave balls in this building, which was

Above, La Redoute, a splendid setting for state occasions; right, the Theaterplatz; on the right-hand page, a fountain in Godesberg's Kurpark, and the 'Mother Earth' tomb in the castle cemetery.

also used for concerts, ballet performances and games of hazard.

The villages around the town have largely remained unspoilt by redevelopment. Muffendorf, which existed in Carolingian times, has retained the aspect of a sizable half-timbered settlement dating from the 17th to 19th centuries. On a hill not far from the main road stands the old Martinskirche, a Romanesque church from the late 12th century, raised on the site of a Roman temple dedicated to Diana, goddess of the chase.

Mehlem is not only the southernmost part of the Bonn district, but its limits towards the Rhine are also the border between Rhineland-Palatinate and Rhineland-Westphalia. The Mainzer Strasse is edged by grand villas, and the Drachenstein park offers unique views over the Rhine to the Drachenfels.

Left, the Drachenfels, seen from Drachenstein park in Mehlem; above, half-timbered buildings in Muffendorf and the Romanesque Martinskirche.

Excursions around Bonn

The most popular excursion destination is undoubtedly the Siebengebirge ('seven hills'). Since 1836, some parts of the mostly forested slopes have been protected areas, and in 1923 all 10,000 acres were included in the nature reserve. Thus the Siebengebirge, with its 200 kilometres of pathways, is the oldest nature reserve in Germany. The 'Naturpark Siebengebirge', as it has been officially called since 1958, has been honoured with the European Diploma on several occasions.

The Drachenfels, with a height of 321 metres, compared with the 461-metre-high Ölberg and the 455 metres of the Löwenburg, is among the lowest peaks of the Siebengebirge. It is, nevertheless, the most famous of the seven hills, and with 2.5 million visitors a year, probably the most-climbed hill in the world! Of the once mighty castle, only ruins, of the four-cornered tower remain. Archbishop Arnold of Cologne laid the foundation stone of the

castle at the southernmost edge of his domains in 1147, but soon mortgaged it. Two years later, it was completed by Gerhard von Are, provost of the Bonn Cassius-stift. From 1176 it was the seat of the counts of Drachenfels, who had a dragon in their coat-of-arms. The castle was destroyed in 1634. In the following centuries the ruins were threatened by the nearby stone-quarries. Trachyte was extracted here already in the 13th century for the building of Cologne cathedral, and by the early 19th century the quarries had crept so close to the former castle that it was in danger of collapsing completely. The Prussian government finally bought it, in 1836, and secured it after the quarries were closed. In 1970 further measures became necessary in order to save the Drachenfels castle. A strong concrete reinforcement, unfortunately left visible to visitors, now holds the structure together.

The view from the Drachenfels is one of the broadest and most beautiful on the Rhine. Towards the east are the Siebengebirge, while 260 metres below the peak stretches the wide ribbon of the river, in which the islands of Nonnenwerth and Grafenwerth lie like ships at anchor. Opposite rise the Rod-

derberg, the Rolandsbogen and the gentle hills of the lands once ruled from the Drachenfels.

Three traditional paths lead the visitors from Königswinter to the Drachenfels plateau, 30 metres below the summit, where the not universally admired massive concrete building of the hotel-restaurant stands. The best view is obtained from the steep Eselsweg (donkey path) which can be partly ascended on the back of just such an animal.

A path through the Nachtigallental, a cool and damp cleft in the soft tuff, is less strenuous for the walker, but the ravine does not afford a view of the Rhine valley. It winds past the memorial, raised in 1949, to the Cologne author and carnival song-writer Willi Ostermann (1876—1936).

The most pleasant ascent is offered by the rack-railway, built in 1883, and the first of its kind in Germany. Over a distance of 1435 metres it climbs 220 metres, which is equal to a gradient of 20 %. In its century of operation, it has transported over 25 million people. Only once did it make the headlines, in 1958, when the full train became derailed; 17 people were killed and 112 injured in the accident.

Above, the Drachenfels, the most famous peak of the Siebengebirge; above right, Konrad Adenauer's house in Rhöndorf; right, the pavilion where the first Federal Chancellor wrote his memoirs.

Only some two kilometres south of the Drachenfels lies Rhöndorf, which became famous as the home of the first Federal Chancellor, Konrad Adenauer. The Zennis-weg leads from the centre of the village to Adenauer's house, now called the 'Bundes-kanzler-Adenauer-Haus' Foundation. It lies at the foot of Konrad Adenauer hill, thus named in 1966.

In 1933 Adenauer was ousted as mayor of Cologne by the National Socialists, and in 1937 he had the house on the hill built. He himself carried the stones for the terrace through the steep garden, and planted fruit and ornamental trees and 150 roses, his favourite flower. He derived as much pleasure from his plants and garden statues as from the bowling alley, laid in 1959, where he regularly played. In 1964 he moved into the pavilion, in which he wrote his memoirs undisturbed by the outside world. Konrad

Adenauer had not completed them when he died on April 19, 1967, after a short illness. Adenauer's seven children reached an agreement with the Federal Republic of Germany on the establishment of the Foundation and presented the Rhöndorf property, including the buildings and their contents, to it. Since then, everything has been left undisturbed, in memory of the first Chancellor of the Federal Republic. His grave is in Rhöndorf's Waldfriedhof cemetery.

Opposite Rhöndorf, on the left bank of the Rhine, lies Mehlem, from where the Rodderberg nature reserve can be reached. A feature of this region is the 800-metre-wide explosion crater, which originated some 30.000 years ago. Up to 48 metres deep, the

Above, Gudenau castle in the Drachenfelser Ländchen; below, the radio telescope in Wachtberg-Werthoven; right, Rolandsbogen.

hollow is covered by loose fertile soil with the Broichhof in the middle. The border between Bonn and Wachtberg runs east-west across the crater, while the 195-metre-high volcanic peak lies in Rhineland-Palatinate. It is not far from Rodderberg to ivy-clad Rolandsbogen, the remains of a castle of the Cologne electoral princes, built in 1100 and badly damaged in 1633. Rolandsbogen, a favourite subject of Romantic artists, collapsed on New Year's Eve, 1840. However, it was restored in the same year through the

efforts of the political poet Ferdinand Freiligrath, who raised the necessary funds by a poem and collecting donations.

The Rhine-Sieg district, whose administrative centre is Siegburg on the right bank of the Rhine, also encircles the Bonn city limits on the left bank of the river and provides a harmonious transition to the more rugged Eifel region. Numerous castles and palaces give the landscape a particular charm. In the Wachtberg commune alone, there are four well-preserved moated castles. They are private property and can only rarely be visited. A modern addition to the commune, which was formed in 1969 out of 13 villages, is the covered radio telescope of the Research Association for Applied Natural Sciences, near Werthoven, which is used for the obser-

vation of satellites. In neighbouring Berkum is Odenhausen castle, built in 1560, one of the few moated castles at an altitude.

The Drachenfelser Ländchen was ruled for centuries from the moated Gudenau castle near Vilich. This castle, built in about 1200 in the valley of the Godesberg stream, was from 1402 the seat of the counts of Drachenfels, who through the purchase of castles and manorial rights extended their 'Ländchen' (estates) until in 1659 it finally became an independent territory in the Reich.

Adendorf has become famous more for its potteries than its two moated castles. The potters moved here from the Westerwald around the middle of the 17th century since the area provided ample quantities of clay

and the Kottenforst abundant wood for the ovens.

When the late-Romanesque abbey church at Heisterbach was consecrated in 1237, it was the largest church in the Rhineland. Today all that it left of one of the finest examples of 13th-century Rhineland architecture is the ruins of the chancel which still stand to give an impression of its former splendour. The ambulatory with its nine chapels, the ornamented columns and the vaulting supported by powerful buttresses were only preserved because in 1818 a conservation order was placed on the building which, after secularisation in 1809, had been sold for demolition. Brühl, today a town with 50,000 inhabitants, was in the 12th century the administrative centre of the extensive estates of the arch-

On the left-hand page and above, the ruined abbey of Heisterbach; top, the Eifel country-side at Bonn's gates; right, an Adendorf potter at work.

bishops of Cologne. The latter increasingly came into conflict with the prosperous merchants of the city, who sought commercial and political freedom, while the archbishops strove to preserve their temporal overlordship. Archbishop Siegfried von Westerburg (1274—1297) started the building of a moated castle here, which was completed by his successor, Wikbold von Holte (1297—1304). During the occupation of Brühl by the troops of Louis XIV, the mediaeval castle was blown up on April 21, 1689. After the devastations of the French, Elec-

toral Prince Joseph Clement (1688—1723) dedicated himself first of all to the rebuilding of his residence in Bonn. In 1715 he explained to the Parisian court architect, Robert de Cotte, his plan to import the achievements of French architecture but to use the remains of the old castle in order to save on the cost. Also planned was an avenue to Bonn and a canal to the Rhine.

Joseph Clement's nephew and successor, Clement Augustus (1723—1761), had other plans when he decided to construct Augustusburg at Brühl as his favorite residence. He was delighted equally by the beauty of the landscape and the possibilites for falconry, a sport of which this scion of the house of Wittelsbach was passionately fond. Clement Augustus remained true to his uncle's wish to use the remains of the old castle for the building of a new one. He entrusted the task to the Westphalian architect Johann Conrad Schlaun, who planned the three-winged structure, open towards the east, incorporated a heavy round tower at the northwestern corner and built another at the southwest

corner. The electoral residence was completed in 1725, three years after the laying of the foundations.

Because of the criticism of the Bavarian electoral prince Charles Albrecht, Augustusburg failed to retain the appearance of a moated castle. Clement Augustus was persuaded to make a fundamental change in the plans by the Bavarian court architect François de Cuvilliés and his landscape architect Dominique Girard. Schlaun was dismissed and thenceforth worked for the electoral prince only in Westphalia. Under the supervision of Michael Leveilly, the moats were filled in and a large garden was created on the southern side of the castle. For the construction of the magnificent staircase, Clement Augustus engaged the celebrated architect Balthasar Neumann, who stayed in Brühl for the first time in 1740. Between 1747 and 1750 the famous Carlo Carlone painted the ceiling of the staircase with subjects glorifying the electoral princes. Clement Augustus did not live to see the completion of his palace. His successor Max Frederick of Königseck-

Rothenfels (1761—1784) saw Augustusburg finished in 1768, after more than 40 years of work.

When the Cologne electorate fell in 1794 in the turmoil of the French Revolution and French troops occupied the palace, all the furniture was carried off. Napoleon visited Augustusburg in 1804, and five years later gave it to his Marshal Davoust, who allowed it to become run-down. After the castle passed into Prussian hands in 1815, Frederick William IV ordered its restoration, which was finally carried out in 1876—77. The Second World War brought further destruction. The first urgent repairs in 1945 were followed by extensive restoration.

Above right, Augustusburg palace at Brühl; above left, its magnificent staircase by Balthasar Neumann; right, the audience chamber of the Baroque palace.

94

CONTENT

Aknowledgements

Fotografie Bernd Siering, Bonn & Thomas Thelen, Erkrath, alle Aufnahmen außer:

Werbe- und Verkehrsamt der Stadt Bonn, Bonn: Titelbilder, S. 21 m., S. 27 m., S. 46 o.
Informations- u. Presseamt der Bundesregierung, Bonn: S. 25 r.u., S. 26 o. und u., S. 27 u.
Rheinisches Landesmuseum, Bonn S. 11, S. 36: Damm/Zefa S. 95

Luftbilder: Freigeg. Reg. Präs. Düsseldorf, S. 58 0A 1470, S. 74 0A 1471, S. 28/29
0A 1472, S. 80/81 0A 1473, S. 48 0A 1474, S. 16 0A 1475, S. 57 0A 1476, S. 49
0A 1477, S. 31 0A 1478

Important Dates

13-9 BC

According to the Roman writer Florus, the Romans built a ship-bridge over the Rhine between 'Bonna' and 'Gesonia'. This is the first mention of Gensem on the right bank of the Rhine. While there are some scholars who have placed Florus's bridge elsewhere, it seems indisputable that the Romans did have a bridgehead to the north of present-day Bonn before Anno Domini.

AD 96

The Roman legion camp in the north of the present city is first mentioned, by Tacitus, as *Castra Bonnensia*. Destruction of the camp during the uprising of the Batavi, a Germanic tribe from the mouth of the Rhine, followed by rebuilding of the fort.

804

First mention of the *Villa Basilica* near the Münster, the centre of the mediaeval and present-day city. In the area of the former camp, only the so-called Dietkirche, the southern part of Bonnburg, is inhabited in Frankish time.

921

Meeting of Kings Henry I and Charles the Simple on a ship anchored at Bonn in order to draw up a peace treaty. As a result, Lotharingia and Bonn become part of the German Kingdom.

c. 978

Founding of Vilich abbey. The first abbess, daughter of the founders, is revered as a saint soon after her death. From this period dates the 'Pützchens Markt' fair.

c. 1000

Shift of the centre of gravity from the Roman camp area to the Münster settlement, which acquires the name of 'Bonn'.

10th—11th centuries

The *Villa Basilica* with the Cassiusstift abbey (near the presumed graves of the city patrons Cassius and Florentius) becomes the *Stiftsburg* (episcopal town).

c. 1150

Large part of the Münster built during the time of Provost Gerhard von Are.

1151

Consecration of St Clement's at Schwarzrheindorf, one of the most remarkable Romanesque churches in Germany because of its two-storey structure and well-preserved wall painting.

1198

King Philip of Swabia burns the city during his campaign against King Otto the Guelph and Archbishop Adolf of Cologne.

1210

Building of Godesburg castle by Archbishop Dietrich I as the archbishopric's bastion to the south.

1244

Archbishop Konrad von Hochstaden fortifies the city and gives the inhabitants citizens' rights and freedom. The Stiftsburg at the Münster, fortified earlier, is enclosed in the city walls.

1288

Archbishop Siegfried von Westerburg grants the city the right to choose a twelve-man council.

1314

Frederick III the Fair of Austria is crowned German king in the Münster by Archbishop Heinrich von Virneburg.

1346

Coronation of Charles IV by Archbishop Walram in the Bonn Münster.

1542

Archbishop Hermann von Wied tries to establish the reformation in Bonn with the help of Martin Bucer. He is defeated by Emperor Charles V, and forced to abdicate in 1547.

1544

The *Bonner Gesangbüchlein* (Bonn hymn-book) is published by Lorenz van der Mülen, and becomes the basis of the unified reformed hymn-book.

1583—87

Reformation attempt by Elector-Archbishop Gebhard Truchsess von Waldburg, who became a Protestant, married, and tried to turn the Cologne archbishopric into a secular principality. In 1583, during the war of Cologne (1583—1588), the troops of the newly-elected Archbishop, Ernest of Bavaria, a Wittelsbach, destroy Godesburg and occupy Bonn.

1587

Bonn is taken by forces loyal to Gebhard Truchsess, led by Martin Schenk von Nideggen.

1601

Ferdinand, politically the most important Wittelsbach to rule in Cologne, moves the electoral residence to Bonn and proceeds with the Counter-Reformation.

1689

Destruction of the fortified city during its occupation by troops under Elector Frederick II of Brandenburg.

1715

Demolition of Bonn's fortifications at the request of the Netherlands. Beginning of the construction of Baroque electoral residences, the Stadtschloss and Poppelsdorf palace, by Joseph Clement (1687—1723) continued by Clement Augustus (1723—1761).

1770

Birth of Bonn's favourite son, Ludwig van Beethoven, in the house which is now No. 20 Bonngasse. In 1792 he moved to Vienna where he died in 1827.

1786

Elector Max Francis of Habsburg-Lotharingia, son of the Austrian Empress Maria Theresa, raises the Bonn Academy, founded in 1777, to the level of a university.

1790

Max Francis builds up the Godesberg mineral spring, known to the Romans. Construction of bathing and social establishments, among them La Redoute.

1794

French Revolutionary troops occupy Bonn, which is held by France until 1814. The University is suppressed.

1815

Bonn comes into the possession of Prussia, which makes the garrison part of the administration of the Rhine Province.

1818

After fierce competition with Cologne, the Rheinische Friedrich-Wilhelms-Universität is founded. Ernst Moritz Arndt, August Wilhelm Schlegel and Georg Niebuhr are among its first professors.

1840

Gottfried and Johanna Kinkel founded the 'Maikäferbund', a society of younger Rhine Romantics, among them Wolfgang Müller von Königswinter, Emanuel Geibel and Ferdinand Freiligrath.